BRIGHT IDEAS

Inspirations for BECOMING A READER

Published by Scholastic
Publications Ltd,
Villiers House,
Clarendon Avenue,
Leamington Spa,
Warwickshire CV32 5PR

© 1992 Scholastic Publications Ltd

Reprinted 1992

Written by Diana Bentley, Dee Reid
and Sylvia Karavis
Edited by Christine Lee
Sub-edited by Catherine Baker
Designed by Lynne Joesbury and
Liz Harrison
Series designed by Juanita
Puddifoot
Illustrated by Linzi Henry
Cover design by Lynne Joesbury
Cover artwork by Caroline Porter

Designed using Aldus Pagemaker
Processed by Pages Bureau,
Leamington Spa
Artwork by Norfolk House
Graphics, Leicester
Printed in Great Britain by
Ebenezer Baylis & Son, Worcester

**British Library Cataloguing in
Publication Data**
A catalogue record for this book is
available from the British Library.

ISBN 0-590-53008-9

CONTENTS

Introduction

'Reading is much more than the decoding of black marks upon a page: it is a quest for meaning and one which requires the reader to be an active participant.' (DES/WO 1989a.)

Reading is making meaning from print. It might be easier to get closer to an understanding of the real nature of reading by deciding what is not reading.

For example, even if you don't understand Italian, you might be able to match sounds to the following Italian phrase:

'Lasciate ogni speranza voi che entrate.'*

With practice, you may even be able to say it sufficiently clearly to communicate with an Italian speaker. But would you be reading? No, you would not. Matching sounds to letters is only part of being a reader. If those sounds do not make sense to the reader then no real reading is taking place.

To understand the nature of reading, it is useful to look at some of the ways in which reading has been approached over the years.

*'All hope abandon, ye who enter here.' Dante.

BACKGROUND

The historical overview

'There is no one method, medium, approach, device, or philosophy that holds the key to the process of learning to read.' (DES, 1975.)

The problem of how to teach children to read is not new. All alphabetic scripts seem to present problems to their potential readers. We know that in Ancient Greece one father desperately gave his struggling son twenty-four slaves, each named after one of the letters of the alphabet, but we do not know how effective this was in helping

him to read! Some Romans are said to have made letters out of bread or cakes to help with their recognition, but mostly any failing child was dealt with in the time-honoured way – by corporal punishment. The problem was known – its solution remained a secret.

By the end of the nineteenth century three main approaches to teaching reading had developed. These were the alphabetic method; the look-and-say method (single words and whole sentences); and the phonic method.

The alphabetic method

The oldest of these approaches was the alphabetic method, by which the pupil learned the names of the letters of the alphabet and their order. Children would say the names of the letters in a word and

would then be expected to say the word! As there is very little relationship between the *name* of the letters in a word and the way the word sounds or is finally pronounced, many children found this difficult. Imagine trying to decode a simple word like 'dog' by saying 'dee-oh-gee' and you can see the problem. Those who were successful seem to have been so despite, rather than because of, their ability to say the letter names. Gradually this approach fell from favour, although it was still common in British schools well into the twentieth century.

Strengths
• The alphabetic method encourages letter recognition. There is evidence that knowledge of letter names and the ability to attach them to the correct letter shape is often a good predictor of later reading success.
• It focuses the child's attention upon letter shapes.
• It encourages left to right orientation.
• The alphabetic method can be helpful in learning some spellings. It is often easier to remember a sequence of letter names than to spell using sounds which are represented in more than one way. For

example, the same sound may be represented by 'ough', 'ow' and 'ou' in different words.

Weaknesses
• The alphabetic method pays minimal attention to the meaning of the words.
• It gives little support for turning the letter names into the letter sounds.
• It appears to be a very slow way to acquire a sight vocabulary.

Look-and-say: the single word approach

The 'look-and-say' or 'whole word' method was almost universally used by the beginning of the twentieth century. Based on the supposedly scientific psychological theory that the whole is easier to perceive than the individual parts, it advocates that teachers should present words as 'wholes' which pupils should then learn to recognise, and subsequently read. Many teachers made large flash cards of the words their pupils were going to meet

in their first readers. They held these out in front of the class and the pupils were then expected to chant out the correct word. Many children did manage this, but others waited a split second and then echoed the words of their more competent peers. Deciding who was doing the saying and who the echoing was a difficult task. To help with this, teachers made smaller word cards for the pupils to take home in tins, and the children were expected to learn these with or without the help of their parents. Again, many children succeeded, but far too many failed because they had no strategies for attacking unknown words. Teachers began to seek an alternative

approach that might help these children.

Strengths
• The single word method often has the effect of boosting a child's confidence if he is already familiar with the words before reading the book.
• It tends to ensure that the reader rarely offers a non-existent word, although she may offer a word which makes nonsense of the text.
• It encourages the child to pay close attention to the look of words, and thus may produce better spellers.

• It allows high-usage words to be quickly absorbed, which aids the reading of many simple texts.

Weaknesses
• The single word method tends to involve learning words in isolation, with little attempt to link word and meaning.
• The rest of the text is often needed to make the meaning of individual words clear, a fact which is not taken into account in the single word method. For example, a child may be able to produce the word 'by' without realising that it means different things in different contexts – 'he went *by* plane', 'she was given the book *by* the teacher'.

• The single word method encourages the child to read 'word by word', in a stilted manner.
• It can lead to individual letters being ignored, which in turn leads to 'wrong' recognition, especially with medial vowels, such as hat/hut.
• It can encourage wild guessing, with the child offering any word as substitute.
• It offers no real attack skills for unknown words.
• It involves considerable reliance upon an adult reader to provide the correct word.
• It uses a restricted vocabulary which produces awkward, stilted texts.

Look-and-say: the whole sentence method

The whole sentence method first appeared around 1870, but it remained a little-used approach until the middle of the twentieth century. It was based on the belief that the sentence was the true unit in reading, just as it is in speaking. A whole sentence allowed the thought to govern the understanding and encouraged natural expression in oral reading. Analysis of individual words came after the understanding of the whole unit. This would appear to be quite 'modern', but it received little support as few publishers were prepared to put such thinking into their reading schemes.

Strengths
• The whole sentence method puts words within whole sentences.
• It uses the child's own sentences for early reading experiences.
• It encourages intonation, expression, phrasing and pitch when reading.
• It takes the child's own knowledge of language as the basis for texts, for example, when the teacher writes the child's own sentences.
• The whole sentence method

usually involves silent reading before oral reading, to enable the child to 'possess thought' before attempting to read aloud.

• It often takes known meaningful texts as a basis, for example, well-known traditional tales and rhymes.

Weaknesses

• The whole sentence method allows and encourages a high percentage of wild guessing.
• It does not encourage or help with word attack skills.
• It uses over-repetitive texts which are dull and mundane.
• It rarely uses stories and offers no incentive for the child to respond to the text.

The phonic method

The phonic approach was based on the belief that if pupils could learn all the 'sounds' that letters, or combinations of letters, made and could then attach them correctly to unknown words, they would quickly become readers. The difficulty lay in deciding how many 'sounds' there were in the English language and then in ensuring the child used the right sound when she looked at the letters. For example, used in conjunction with other letters, the letters 'ho' have the following sounds: hot, hope, hook, hoot, house, hoist, horse, horizon, honey, how, honest. The sound 'sh' can be written using sh (ship), ci (ancient), ti (attention) and ce (ocean). Similarly, 'two vowel' combinations were the downfall of many young pupils.

One reading scheme from the 1960s and 70s was so concerned with providing practice with short vowels, it became oblivious to the meaning of the sentences that were constructed; for example: 'Mum met ten men in Pat's tent'! (Gattegno, 1970.)

This kind of text encouraged children to concentrate on the 'external' form of the words rather than to respond to the meaning behind the words (perhaps just as well in the case of the above quotation!).

This approach has continued to have its followers, and perhaps is most clearly seen in the Initial Teaching Alphabet, where all the words of the early readers were written in a purely phonetic way.

'Sally's muther sed, "hav yw pwt on ywr coet, Sally?" Sally pwt on her coet. Sally and her muther waukt tw scwl.' (Downing, 1963.)

Strengths

• The phonic method enables the child to 'attack' unknown words.
• It enables the child to make a good attempt at spelling words.
• It is an important part of spelling development.

bit but bat

THE BRITISH ISLES

• It focuses the child's attention on to the letters and words of texts.
• It has been shown to produce higher reading scores on word and sentence reading tests.
• It ensures that the child doesn't have to wait to be told unknown words; generally he is able to make a reasonable attempt.
• There has been some evidence of early sustained reading ability from children who master these sounds.

Weaknesses

• The phonic method pays little attention to the meaning of words.
• It does not allow for the fact that some letters such as 'a', in combination with others, represent many sounds.

• It does not allow for the fact that some 'sounds' are represented by many different letter combinations.
• A child who moves to a different part of the country, where words are pronounced differently, may be confused by apparent inconsistencies.
• The phonic method tends to involve stilted and artificial texts.
• It blends letters together in a way which is very difficult for many children.
• It encourages children to offer nonsense words if they have learned phonic attack skills isolated from meaning.

Where did the old schemes go wrong?

'Teachers should recognise that reading is a complex but unitary process and not a set of discrete skills which can be taught separately in turn and, ultimately, bolted together.' (DES/WO, 1988.)

Apart from using unnatural language which made texts difficult to predict, old-style reading schemes also gave children confusing messages about the reading process. Instead of using one word as a clue to the meaning of the next, children were generally expected to treat each word in isolation and each word had to be remembered individually.

This often restricted children's reading ability to the extent of their visual memory. It also encouraged children to treat each word as a code to be cracked without giving them the benefit of other contextual clues. Competent readers draw upon a host of clues when making meaning out of print. Don Holdaway effectively illustrates this when he gives the following sentence to be read:

'Lextexx xxx xox xxe oxxy xluxx xo uxxxown xoxxs.'* (The Foundations of Literacy, 1979).

Most people can read this line, even though many of the letters have been removed. This is because, in addition to the evidence of our eyes, we also read what our brain

*'Letters are not the only clues to unknown words.'

expects to be there from all the other contextual clues. A similar exercise with the text from an early reading scheme proves very difficult indeed:

'Cxxx, xxxe, xoxx, ux, xx, xp.'*

Children who have become over-dependent upon phonic building, or a sight vocabulary, believing it to be a prerequisite for reading any word, can actually fail to respond to the content of the text. The sheer mechanics of 'sounding it out' tends to dominate the process at the expense of the child responding to the *meaning* behind the blended sounds.

If we encourage children to make sense of their reading, we must make available simple texts that *do* make sense.

Some recent approaches

Behind all these methods one can see the seeds of today's thinking, and the origins of practices both good and bad which are still found in our schools. Unfortunately, after the Second World War many schemes concentrated on technique at the expense of meaning. In the 1980s a new approach developed in reaction to the stilted, dull and frequently almost meaningless texts of many reading schemes.

The psycholinguistic method

The psycholinguistic or 'real book' method took into consideration the vast amount of research which illustrated the importance of building upon the knowledge about print that children bring to school. During the 1980s there was a dramatic increase in the publication of stunning picture books written by outstanding authors. This provided the

materials that the 'real book' approach needed in order to entice children into the world of literature.

The psycholinguistic approach emphasises that texts should be both meaningful and interesting to the reader and rejects the teaching of reading through graded schemes or by giving children a series of books offered in a hierarchical order. Only when children understand the real purpose of reading are they ready to tackle print. As with all the other approaches, this too has had its successes and failures.

Strengths
• The psycholinguistic approach shows the child the real purpose for reading.
• It lets the child experience high quality texts.
• It tends to create readers for life rather than just enabling children to read.
• It emphasises understanding and responding to the text before decoding.
• It encourages children to use prediction as a means of attacking unknown words.
• It familiarises children with well-written texts which can later be reflected in their own writing.
• It invites teachers to find out about children's literature.

*'Come, come, come, up, up.'

• It demonstrates to children that reading involves interpretation beyond the literal.
• It allows the child to develop useful criteria for selecting books, for example, by author, interest and recommendation, rather than depending on a coloured label, a level or a number.

Weaknesses
• The psycholinguistic approach often allows children to think they can create the text without needing to read the words.
• It allows the child to over-rely on the pictures rather than the text.
• It makes a sight vocabulary slower to achieve due to a lack of repetition in the texts.
• It can be daunting to some readers because of the wide variation in the texts.
• It may baffle the young reader because of the complexity of the text.
• It may make it difficult for children initially to select books unless the teacher spends considerable time giving individual advice.

Using a combination

Of course, many teachers and schools use a combination of several approaches, trying to match the method with the strengths of the individual child. This becomes easier when the resources within the school depend less upon a single scheme, and books are chosen with a wide variety of both subject matter and approach. It was seeing this in action that persuaded the HMIs to praise those schools which used a mix of reading schemes and books, and which were able to match the child with the book effectively.

How has thinking changed?

The importance of making sense
More recent thinking has recognised the role of both phonic clues and a sight vocabulary in becoming a reader, while acknowledging the necessity to foster these skills within the context of a passage which is interesting to the child and which, above all, makes sense.

The child's perception of reading
Some children have a very different perception of the reading process from that of teachers. As competent readers themselves, teachers have a clear idea about *why* they are reading. Most importantly, they expect what they are reading to make sense. Not all children approach the reading task with such clear motives and expectations. For some

children, the strategies of word decoding can actually get in the way of making sense of what they read. If we compare reading with completing a jigsaw it is obvious that fitting all the necessary pieces together is only possible if we have a clear idea of what we expect the finished picture to look like. When they start reading, many children are given the individual pieces of the reading jigsaw (phonics, word recognition and so on) without being shown the picture on the box! It is not that phonic or visual clues are unimportant. They are very important, but not at the expense of the most important strategy – a desire to make *sense* of the words read.

The importance of good books

Over the past few years there has been a great increase in literature published for children. Earlier approaches to reading used literature as the reward for children once they had mastered the 'mechanics' of reading. More recent approaches have offered children quality fiction while they are in the process of acquiring the techniques of reading.

The benefits of good stories are the same for children as they are for any reader:
• a feeling of having been engaged in a worthwhile task;
• a challenge to the mind and heart;
• the enrichment of good language;
• the desire to reread.
All these are the entitlement of the young reader.

It would, of course, be a naïve teacher who imagined that literature alone made children become readers, but while it is not the only influence, it is an important aspect that cannot be excluded.

'Real books'

The polarisation of the argument between real books and reading schemes has done little to assist the busy teacher. What makes a book real is when children have chosen it for its content and not for its colour coding; when they have had some choice in the selection of the book and when it has given them some pleasure. (It is worth remembering that a child's pleasure in a text may surprise us; children's perceptions of what is a good book often differ from adults' ideas on the subject.) There are plenty of excellent stories available within reading schemes, just as there is plenty of expensive hardback fiction which is a waste of money. The expensive packaging does not guarantee quality.

Conclusion

It would be over-simplistic to think that all the approaches discussed in this chapter neatly followed one after the other. In reality they all waxed and waned in popularity and many schools have undoubtedly used a little of each. Indeed, in 1924 Smith and Courtis published a scheme called 'The Picture Story Reading Lessons'. This, they claimed, would enable all children who followed it exactly to learn to read. It consisted of two story books (77 pages and 154 pages!), two teacher's manuals (212 pages and 209 pages!), a picture dictionary and a work book.

The instructions for the teacher were impressive: labels were to be put around the classroom for the children to read, the teacher was to demonstrate the direction of print when reading to the class, a lesson should include games and, above all, the individual progress of the child should be monitored. The system worked initially through the telling of stories, the children then taking part in improvised drama, reading the plays and finally writing about the story. It continued by offering the children graded stories and later reading for

different purposes. It incorporated word attack methods, progress charts and more activities! This was a remarkable scheme that was the forerunner of many of today's reading schemes.

In conclusion, we know that no single approach will teach all children to read, but every approach, however bizarre, has taught someone to read.

In her seminal work *Learning to Read: The Great Debate*, Chall shows that zeal and success often follow a 'new' approach. Teachers who are enthusiastic about their subject and who are prepared to try something different, whatever it is, achieve results. The 'new approach' they adopt frequently emphasises something that their previous practice has ignored or underemphasised. Above all, teachers who have thought about the reasons for their approach produce the confident readers that every school desires.

In 1990, an HMI report on standards of reading in the United Kingdom said:

'The effective teaching of reading calls for skill and knowledge to be applied consistently and with sufficient flexibility to ensure that children benefit from the appropriate method at the right time. Successful teaching of reading in the majority of schools used a mix of methods, each reinforcing the other as the children's reading developed.' (DES, 1990a.)

As teachers of young children, we must be aware of the stage of understanding and development that a child has reached, and then decide on appropriate action. The match between the child, the text and the diagnosis by the teacher is crucial if we are to enable young children to make fast and effective advances in reading.

CHAPTER 1

Introducing reading

'When people explained their past with stories, told themselves the present with stories, foretold the future with stories, the best place by the fire was kept for... the Storyteller.' (Minghella, 1988.)

Story-telling has been important to the human race since civilization began. Traditionally, all cultures have revered the story-teller. In our present culture, however, stories have become enshrined in books and the tradition of telling stories has declined. Of course, reading stories aloud is still a priority in many schools and homes, but this is not quite the same as telling stories.

BACKGROUND

Story-telling

Story-telling is a very direct form of communication. It requires the teller to take account both of the tale and of the audience. In this way, it marries the two more perfectly than a written story. Story-telling reaches out to the audience and makes contact with them.

Story-telling encourages children to see themselves as story-tellers. This is very important, as much of our conversation is in the form of mini-stories. We recount details of our lives, and our experiences are woven into our stories. Children need to acquire this fundamental grammar of thought and expression.

Story-telling enables adults to place the children who listen to the story at the centre of the tale. They become the heroes and heroines of the adventures, and are thus connected with the story. This can enhance their sense of their own value and importance. During story-telling sessions, the teacher can tell stories about the school and about places and people in it. There is much psychological evidence to suggest that children need to have in their heads a clear 'map' which indicates their relationship to others as well as their geographical location in the school.

What kind of stories can we tell?

It is very important to tell children stories about their school. Telling stories entitled 'When the refuse collectors come to our school' not only helps children understand something about their local environment, but also gives them some very useful vocabulary. Stories with fairly mundane details about the lives of those who work in the school may, on the surface, seem uninteresting to young children, but we are all more interested in other people's lives than we may care to admit (witness the popularity of soap operas with young children).

Some possible titles of stories to help children 'map' their world both geographically and psychologically are as follows:
• What does the school cook do each day?
• Where do the library books come from?
• What happens if you fall over in the playground?
• What happens in the school after all the children have gone home?
• What does the school secretary do?

Other potential titles grouped thematically could be as follows:

School
• The caretaker and the hamster;
• The day the keys got lost;
• The day the lorry got stuck;
• The missing sandwiches;
• The day it snowed;
• Mrs — the lollipop lady;
• School dinners;
• The monster in the playground.

Animals
• The naughty puppy;
• My cat has kittens;
• I want a pet;
• The unusual pet;
• Who left the cage door open?

Festivals
• My best present ever;
• The birthday that was forgotten;
• The birthday in hospital;
• Festival food;
• The fancy dress costume;
• Harvest festival;
• The festival of light;
• Bonfire night.

Helping the beginning reader

Some of the best stories for telling aloud feature definite patterns of rhyme and repetition. Often stories with which the audience is already familiar can be made newly interesting by the direct telling. Stories with a repetitive refrain allow the audience to share in the telling and this can be a very satisfactory partnership.

When a tale is being told there is very little time for listeners to reflect or to predict. The 'natural breaks' provided by repetitive refrains such as 'I'll huff and I'll puff...' give the *teller* a moment to prepare the rest of the story and the *listeners* the opportunity to step back momentarily from the action and to cast their minds back over previously recounted events. Young children can be actively encouraged to engage in this activity. Involvement in the unfolding of a story helps children to use the most important of cueing strategies – predicting words and phrases based on an understanding of the story.

When telling the children a story with a repetitive refrain it is useful if the refrain is written out in large clear writing on a board or flipchart. This helps young readers to make a vital connection between the spoken word and its written form. When those words occur in your story, draw the children's attention to them using a pointer. This not only encourages audience participation in the story but it fixes in children's minds the concept of words as separate units of meaning in written form – a distinction which is not evident in spoken language. (Many adults may have learned a phrase in a foreign language which they are able to *say* accurately, but they may be very surprised to see how it is constituted in words. In the same way, many children think you write 'Oncer ponatime' rather than 'Once upon a time'.)

When you are both the creator and the teller of a story you have complete mastery over its plot and its delivery. As a story-teller one can break off from the action at any suitable moment and invite the audience to comment or to predict what might happen next. Of course, one can always do this when reading aloud to a class, but the advantage of story-telling is that one can decide what *does* happen next, depending upon contributions made by the group.

Starting and ending

Story-telling benefits from careful signalling. When we read from a book we have the benefit of pages being turned to signify the progress of the story. We can see the number of pages we have read and the number of pages still to come. On an even simpler level, merely by holding a book we can indicate that a story is to be told. Of course, in oral story-telling, all these cues are absent. In order to assist the audience to be prepared for what is to come it is very useful to have a few stock opening rhymes to help focus the mind of the audience before the story-telling starts.

We are all familiar with the opening 'Once upon a time...', but this way of capturing the attention of listeners has been hijacked by so many written stories that it no longer has quite the magical attraction and promise of secret worlds that it must once have had. It is probably best to invent opening (and closing) rhymes that you and the class have worked out together, but some of the following might prove useful:

• Now I'll tell you a story, and this story is new,
So you listen carefully, and do as I do.
• I'll count down to one and my story's begun,
5, 4, 3, 2, 1.
• Onery, twoery, trickery bell
Sit down quickly
I've a story to tell.
• I'll tell you a story about Jackanory
And now my story's begun.
• Fee fi fo fum,
Now my story has begun.
• Pat your head and rub your tum,
Now my story has begun.

Stories also need little rhymes to indicate the end of the session:
• Pat your head and rub your tum,
Now my story is all done.
• That's the end of the tale,
And the tail is the end of the cat. (You could sometimes change this, perhaps to 'tiger'.)
• Snick snack snickery snend,
Now my story has come to an end.

ACTIVITIES

1. Encouraging story-telling

Age range
Five to six.

Group size
The whole class, initially working in small groups.

What you need
No special equipment.

What to do
Apart from telling stories to the class ourselves we need to encourage the children to become tellers of tales in their own right. To give children the confidence to do this they need:
• a role model;
• prompts for simple one-line 'stories'.

Organise the children in small groups of three or four and allow them to retell stories they have heard you tell. For example, if you have recently told the children a story on a theme such as 'something lost' or 'something found', ask the children to take it in turns within their groups to say, 'One day I lost...'. When each child in each group has told her 'story', ask the groups each to combine with another group and once again let each child tell her story. Continue this process until the whole class forms one group.

Reverse the process by encouraging the children to start off the next story 'One day I found...' in the whole class group before dividing down to smaller groups.

2. Opening lines

Age range
Five to seven.

Group size
The whole class.

What you need
No special equipment.

What to do
Ask all the children to try to think of an opening line for a story. Explain that you are going to count to 60 and, while you do so, they must try to tell every other child in the classroom what their opening line is. For younger children, it is advisable to give the class part of an opening line as an example to start them off, such as 'In the dark, dark, wood I met a ...'. Older children will probably not need this prompt.

Let the children move around and tell every other child the opening line of their

story while you count. When you have finished counting, collect all the children together and ask them which of the opening lines would make them want to hear more of the story. Support and encourage the children whose stories are chosen to elaborate upon their beginning line.

This will encourage children to develop an awareness of audience needs when telling (or writing) a story.

3. Build-a-story 1

Age range
Five to seven.

Group size
The whole class.

What you need
No special equipment.

What to do
Give the children the opening line of a story. Keep it simple at this stage, for example, 'One day I went for a walk'. Invite the children to ask you questions about *where* you went; *who* you met; *what* you did. Each time you accept a suggestion from the class, repeat the story so far, including the new bit of detail. For example:
Teacher: One day I went for a walk in a wood. I wonder what kind of wood it was?
Child: A dark, dark wood.
Teacher: Good. One day I went for a walk in a dark, dark wood. I wonder who I met?
Child: A little old man.
Teacher. Oh, yes. One day I went for a walk in a dark, dark wood and I met a little old man. What was he doing?

Sometimes children fall into the trap of always asking 'What

happened then?' This parallels their habit of writing stories in which all the action is linked by 'and then'. To help children avoid this, ask questions that encourage the children to connect the story with causes and effects ('this happened *because*' and 'the *result* of this was') rather than just temporal sequencing.

4. Build-a-story 2

Age range
Five to seven.

Group size
The whole class or smaller groups.

What you need
No special equipment.

What to do
Initiate a dialogue with the children so that they take an active part in making up a story. For example:
Teacher: What shall we have in our story today?

Class: A monster... a dragon... a lost toy...
Teacher: Well, we had a story about a monster yesterday and a dragon is a kind of monster, so I think that today's story will be about a lost toy. What kind of toy should it be?
Class: A teddy... a cuddly toy... a kite...
Teacher: We heard the story of Dogger on the story tape yesterday, so we won't have another story so soon about a soft toy, but I rather like the idea of a lost kite. Let's have our story about a lost kite.

Continue accepting contributions from the class in this way until a whole story has been built up. Obviously, not all contributions can be incorporated, but make sure you provide an explanation or the promise of being included

6. Pass-the-story

Age range
Five to seven.

Group size
The whole class or smaller groups.

What you need
No special equipment.

What to do
Start to tell the children a story. At an appropriate moment, point at a child and ask him to continue the story. When that child has made a contribution, let him point to another child for the story to be passed on.

When doing this activity with younger children it is best to ensure that the story returns to you from time to time to help you to keep it on track and to ensure that every child has the opportunity to contribute. If the children always choose who is to speak next, you may find that some children only select their friends and other children will not be chosen at all.

If young children find it difficult to build a logical story in this way you can assist them by recapping on the story between the contributions. For example:

Teacher: One day I arrived at school and there was a strange thing in the playground.
Child: It was a spaceship and there were funny green men running around beside it.
Teacher: So I looked at this mysterious spaceship and the funny green men in our playground and I said...

As a variation, the story can be passed around the group in the order in which the children are sitting.

next time for the ones you reject.

Make a point of repeating the story each time a new addition is made to the plot. This will help to keep the children's attention upon the plot. Encourage the class to help you with the repetition, cumulatively building the story much as one would play 'Granny went to market'.

5. Points of view

Age range
Six to seven.

Group size
The whole class.

What you need
No special equipment.

What to do
This activity encourages children to build upon the knowledge they have acquired from repeated retellings of stories, but it also alerts them to all the other possible stories that lurk behind every central story. In terms of understanding story structure it enables children to realise that not every character needs to be fully developed but, on the other hand, the main characters need to be presented with continuity.

Choose a story with which the children are already familiar. Briefly remind the class of the plot of the story. Encourage the children to consider characters who appear in the story but who have only a small part, or characters who never actually appear but who, we presume, must exist, such as Goldilocks's mother and father or the farmer who owned the three Billy Goats Gruff. Ask the children to help you to tell the tale from the point of view of one of these shadowy characters.

7. Sound effects

Age range
Five to seven.

Group size
The whole class.

What you need
No special equipment.

What to do
Before the activity, prepare a story which will require plenty of sound effects. A good example is the nursery song 'We're Going on a Bear Hunt' in which the hunt takes you through squelchy mud, long grass, deep water and so on, all with suitable sound effects.

The first time you do this activity with the children, make the sound effects yourself and encourage the children to follow your example. Once they begin to understand the idea of providing suitable noises, let them make them at appropriate moments in a story which you have made up. Start with a simple tale, such as a visit to the farm, which might begin as follows:
Teacher: Yesterday I was very lucky, I went to visit a farm. I saw a big barn and on the ground was lots of yellow straw and inside the barn were four big black and white... cows.
Children: Mooo, Mooo!

Round off your story in such a way as to make the children run quickly through all the sound effects in turn. For example, if your story is on a farm theme, you could finish by saying goodbye to all the animals.

8. Oral cloze

Age range
Five to seven.

Group size
The whole class.

What you need
No special equipment.

What to do
Oral cloze is identical to a written cloze procedure except that the story is heard rather than read. Tell the class a story, leaving gaps for the children to fill in.

At first, only leave gaps in places where the word to be supplied is fairly obvious. For example:
'This is a story called "The Big Wave". James picked up his bucket and spade. He was very excited. He was spending his holiday at the.... His Gran and... lived near the sea and James loved playing on the beach. He liked to dig with his... and put the sand in his....'

Of course, it is possible to fill in those few gaps with different words, all of which might be considered 'correct', but the important thing is that children search for a good word to fill the gap. Hearing other alternative suitable words will widen their vocabulary and help them to appreciate the variety of language available to us.

Accept all the contributions and gently suggest why some may be unsuitable and why others might be good words but not necessarily the best. Encourage the group to strive to supply the best word in the context.

Swish! rustle! slurp! squelch!

CHAPTER 2

Reading the environment

Not all reading is found between the covers of a book. As literate members of society, we are surrounded by a world of print that communicates its message to us. Children, too, notice this print and seek to understand its message long before they arrive at school. In fact, for many children print in the environment, on shop signs, advertisements, traffic signs, packaging and so on, is their first initiation into the symbolic importance of print. Teachers can build upon this early interest and

awareness and use labels, notices and captions in the classroom to involve children in the reading process. However, it is worth taking a tip from advertising copy-writers and ensuring that the message is eye-catching.

To help children make the connection between a label or notice and its purpose, discuss beforehand whether a label would be useful, where to position it, and what should be written. In this way the children will feel

in control of the print in the classroom environment. There is a danger otherwise that your notices will be nothing more than inconspicuous wallpaper!

Parents can be encouraged to alert their children to the uses of print in the environment. Some parents would not think of pointing out signs and labels to their young child unless encouraged to do so by a teacher.

ACTIVITIES

1. Reading signs

Age range
Five to seven.

Group size
The whole class.

What you need
Cardboard, scissors, felt-tipped pens, Blu-Tack.

What to do
Discuss with the whole class the way signs are used. Can they recognise any, such as shop signs or road signs?

Ask the children where in the classroom signs would be useful. Make some signs on cardboard and stick them up around the classroom. The signs could comprise courtesy messages such as:

- Please close the door.
- Please keep our book corner tidy.

Tell the class what the signs say and remind them about them from time to time. When the children are familiar with the signs, discuss other signs that could be put up in the classroom.

2. Street signs

Age range
Five to seven.

Group size
The whole class.

What you need
Pictures cut from magazines showing shop signs, collage materials, adhesive, scissors, felt-tipped pens, display paper.

What to do
Ask the children to look at the pictures of the signs and help them to read them. Discuss with the class where you might find any of these signs. Ask them why they think signs are important.

Encourage the children to collect pictures of signs or to remember where they have seen signs and draw them in place. These pictures can be made into a collage, or they could be divided into two columns under the headings 'Signs which tell us what to do' and 'Signs which give us information'.

Further activity
Read the 'Thomas the Tank Engine' story which tells what happens when Thomas decides to ignore a 'Stop' sign (Awdry, 1952).

3. Take notice

Age range
Five to seven.

Group size
The whole class.

What you need
A notice-board, paper, pens, Blu-Tack.

What to do
Put up a notice-board in the classroom exclusively for writing messages to the children. Use the notice-board to display notices about the weather or reminders about schools' broadcasts or forthcoming school events. It could also be a way of communicating with individual

children (for example, 'Emily, I found your gym shoe behind the cupboard').

Further activity
If you have a fairly large metallic area in the classroom, such as a cupboard door, use a set of magnetic letters to write a different greeting to the children each morning.

take it in turns to 'fish'. When a child catches a fish, explain that he must read the instruction and then follow it.

4. Fishing game

Age range
Five to seven.

Group size
Groups of three or four.

What you need
Card, a pen, scissors, paper-clips, adhesive tape, small magnets, string.

What to do
Draw some fish shapes on card and cut them out. Write a simple instruction on each fish, such as 'Stand up' or 'Walk around your chair'. Stick a paper-clip to the underside of each fish with adhesive tape.

   Tie some small magnets on to lengths of string to make simple 'fishing rods'. Give each child a fishing rod and let them

5. Joke board

Age range
Six to seven.

Group size
The whole class.

What you need
A board, paper, felt-tipped pens.

What to do
Use a board as a joke board. Each week write a different joke on the joke board. The best kind of jokes for this game are those which have a question-and-answer format. For example:
Why do birds fly south for the winter?
Because it's too far to walk.

   Put the question on one side of the board in a speech bubble and put the answer on the other side. Encourage the

children to read the joke at the beginning of each week.

   Develop this activity by writing only the first half of the joke on the board and then asking the children to read the joke and either write or tell you the answer.

6. Where would I see this sign?

Age range
Five to seven.

Group size
The whole class.

What you need
Pictures of road signs, shop signs, public information signs, etc. (These could be photographs, pictures or hand-drawn signs.)

followed by bread wrappers, etc. Alternatively you might decide to display them as if they were arranged on supermarket shelves. Ask the children to make labels for the shelves and put the prices on the labels. This could then lead on very satisfactorily to playing shopping games.

Further activity
Discuss how products are advertised on hoardings or on television. It is quite likely that the children will not only recognise the products from television but will also be familiar with the appropriate advertising slogans and jingles. Encourage the children to talk about these and share their experiences.

8. Sign quiz

Age range
Five to six.

Group size
The whole class.

What you need
Wrappers and packets from food and sweets.

What to do
Make a pile of the wrappers, then hold them up one by one and ask the children to identify

What to do
Hold up a sign and ask the group 'What does this sign mean?' Repeat this with different signs until all the children are familiar with all the signs, then change the question to 'Where would I see this sign?' Let the children take it in turns to ask the questions.

7. Labels and packaging

Age range
Five to seven.

Group size
The whole class.

What you need
Display materials, an assortment of packaging and labels from household goods. (It is probably best to avoid labels from tins, as there is always a possibility of traces of food being on the label which might cause hygiene problems.)

What to do
Over the course of a few weeks, ask the children to bring in labels and packaging from an assortment of household goods. Help them to sort the packaging into groups; for example, all the toothpaste cartons together. Encourage the children to read what is written on the packaging.

Discuss with the class how best to display the labels. For example, you might decide to arrange them according to their use on a normal day, so that breakfast cereal packets are followed by toothpaste packets, which are followed by drink cartons, which are

them. At first, the children might only be able to identify the wrapper as, for example, a cereal packet. Encourage them to try to read what is written on the packaging.

When the children can readily identify the wrappers, hold them up with only the brand name showing. Encourage the children to say the name of the product. Use this opportunity to draw attention to the names on the wrappers, for example, 'Here is a label which starts with the letter...'. This can then be developed into letter matching games. For example, 'Can anyone else see another label that starts with the same letter?'

Use this game to draw children's attention to capital and lower case letters. Many labels are written in capital letters and you can talk to children about this, suggesting reasons why this might be so. In this way the children can start to appreciate that we use different forms of letters depending upon the needs of the writer.

9. Welcome sign

Age range
Five to seven.

Group size
The whole class.

What you need
Several pieces of A3 paper or card, felt-tipped pens,

What to do
Discuss with the class the importance of making everyone welcome in the classroom. Explain that you are going to write a notice to welcome anyone who comes to visit, such as parents, children from other classes or other teachers. Discuss with the children what you are going to put on the sign. Remind them that signs need to be clear and uncluttered if they are going to be informative. Talk to the children about visitors who might not be able to read a sign in English. Decide how the sign can make them feel welcome too.

Write a clear sign on A3 card or paper, saying, for example, 'Welcome to our school'. Write this same message in other languages on the other pieces of paper or card, enlisting the help of parents if necessary. Display the signs around the classroom, encouraging the children to help you choose where to place them.

10. Writing notes

Age range
Five to seven.

Group size
One or two children at a time.

What you need
Small pieces of paper, a variety of writing implements.

What to do
From time to time write short messages to individual children instead of making a spoken comment. These notes can ask questions ('Is your jumper new, Gary?'). You can also use the notes to praise a

child, either for some very pleasing work or for behaving well.

Of course, many of the children in the class will not be able to read the note for themselves, but by writing to them you are emphasising the importance of reading and writing as a means of communication. Let them bring the note to you so that you can read it to them. Try to draw attention to some detail in the note, for example, the child's name.

11. The 'I can...' chart

Age range
Five to six.

Group size
The whole class.

What you need
A large piece of card, felt-tipped pens.

What to do
Use a felt-tipped pen to divide a large piece of card into four columns. At the top of the piece of card write the words 'I can'. Above each column write

heading; for example:
• tie my tie;
• tie my shoelaces;
• change quickly for PE;
• take a message.

Discuss with the class the purpose of the chart. Enter each child's name as they prove they can complete the task. It is best to do this activity when many children can satisfactorily perform the tasks. It is also important to have at least one activity that *every* child can easily achieve.

12. Captions for pictures

Age range
Five to seven.

Group size
The whole class.

What you need
Card for making labels and captions, pens.

What to do
Sometimes when children's work is displayed the children themselves have no idea of the title of their work because the caption was written by the teacher and not in their presence.

When the children have done some work which you intend to display, discuss what caption or title would be suitable to draw attention to the work. Let the children see you write the caption.

When the caption is in place, encourage the children to read it aloud with you.

I can			
Tie my Shoelaces	Tie my tie	Put my chair up	Take a message
Sarah Tom Chi	Ana Sorinder Lisa	Cathy Chi Sorinder Tom Ana	Tom S

CHAPTER 3

Big books

Many experts agree that big books have become increasingly valuable as a means of involving children in the act of reading. By reading a big book to the class or group, the teacher is able to model reading and to demonstrate how the print on the page becomes the story being told.

In a big book, text and illustrations can be seen clearly by a group of children. Don Holdaway (1979) has suggested that the print size should be clearly visible from approximately 15 feet. It is not only the print that needs to be clearly visible, however. It is equally important that the illustrations are not too busy and can be easily interpreted. Some illustrations that work well in a standard sized book are not effective when enlarged. The kind of illustration which requires children to pore over small details is inappropriate in the big book format.

BACKGROUND

If children are to become confident readers who not only know how to read but are also intellectually and emotionally bound up in the reading process, then 'book experience should precede word experience' (Martin and Brogan, 1972). Using big books as early reading material gives children a perfect introduction to book experience.

Why use big books?

When using a big book, a teacher is able to demonstrate many of the features of reading, such as the left-to-right directionality of print and the way in which the reader follows from the line end to the beginning of the next line. Most importantly, she is able to demonstrate the link between the spoken word and its representation in written form. Many children arrive at the reception class with a very hazy notion about the significance of print. Big books enable even very young children to participate in a 'reading-like' activity.

Initially young children will be unable to read the words on their own. However, with the support of the group and with their guesses confirmed by the teacher's delivery of the text, many will quickly be able to share in the re-creation of the story. As children become familiar with the text, they will be able to use their memories and predictive skills to cue the next word. This can, of course, be helped by the text itself if it employs a predictable rhythm and rhyme. The act of responding and recalling when reading is precisely the response that proficient readers draw on when making meaning of a text.

Unlike their more confident peers, some children will not be able to read in unison with the teacher or even echo her words. What they *can* do is echo their peers' delivery of the text so they are a fraction of a second behind the rest of the group. Although these children are less proficient at remembering words from previous readings they still benefit from being immersed in the reading process, as meaningful words are presented in a context.

Many teachers are familiar with the situation where a child acquires a sight vocabulary but fails to respond to the meaning behind the words. Sometimes, the sheer effort of remembering a word effectively inhibits the child from comprehending its meaning. Within the shared, participatory reading of a big book to the group, there is ample opportunity to examine the meaning behind the words for the benefit of the whole group. The teacher can digress, elaborate upon the text and bring personal experience to bear upon its interpretation – *and so can the children in the group.*

By helping children to make sense of the text through drawing on their existing

knowledge and experience, teachers enable them to learn about the active nature of reading. There is usually insufficient time to share meanings like this in a one-to-one situation.

When using big books with a class or group, the teacher reads aloud the whole story much as an adult at home would share a book with a child. The emphasis is upon enjoying the story and getting as much from it as possible. Many children start school with past experiences of such pleasurable sessions with books. However, other children will not have been so fortunate and a big book session can compensate for their lack of earlier experience of the world of books.

Because of the large format of the books, it is possible to draw attention to features such as the names of the author and illustrator, and to familiarise children with the terminology of books – cover, spine, page number and so on. This will add to children's knowledge about the nature of reading.

Sharing big books combines all the benefits of reading aloud to children with an opportunity for sensitive observation of how they are able to tackle text and interpret story.

Which big books?

There are plenty of big books available from educational publishers. Many of these are big book versions of reading scheme books. Indeed, some reading schemes introduce reading in the big book format. On the whole, these publications are very good, and it is perfectly feasible to use the big books even if the school has no other books from that scheme. Some other big book publications are versions of popular picture books.

It is worth remembering that a big book story will be read by the same children many, many times so it is important that you choose a story that you will *all* still enjoy after multiple rereads! Check, too, that the print size is large enough to be seen by a group of children from a slight distance.

Alternatively, you can make your own big books for your class to read. Often these are most successful when based upon a published book. For

example, if the children have enjoyed the story of Rosie's Walk, they might like you to write a story about 'Angus the bull', who tours the farmyard in much the same way as Rosie does. Of course, with your help, children can make their own big books. They will thus have an added incentive to read them because they themselves will own the text.

Because considerable time and effort, as well as material, goes into producing big books, it is essential that they are used to the best effect. There are good quality texts produced commercially, and although these may sound expensive, they appear cheap when costed against a teacher's time. It is, therefore, not recommended that time is spent producing books that can be bought through a bookshop, such as books of traditional tales or nursery rhymes.

ACTIVITIES

1. How to use big books

Age range
Any age.

Group size
Small groups.

What you need
A big book, an easel or bookstand, a pointer.

What to do
Stand the book on an easel if possible, as holding up a big book for any length of time will make your arms ache! Ensure that all the children in the group can see the book. Before reading the book to the children for the first time, read them the title and talk about the author and illustrator. Encourage the children to speculate about the content of the book. It might be appropriate (for example, when using a non-fiction big book) to develop this speculation by looking through the pictures.

Read the text out loud and use a pointer to help the children to follow the text. Pointing with your finger is insufficiently accurate, as your arm will block out parts of the text for some of the children. It is important to synchronise your pointing with your reading so that what the children hear corresponds with what they see. It is this early grasp of the connection between words spoken and words seen that is one of the dividends of big book reading.

Read the text at a normal pace. There is no need to read slowly, and remember that although your pointer is indicating each word as *you* read it, it is not intended as a test for the children in the group. You are responsible for reading out loud, and the children can join in to speak the words in unison or to echo your words. They are, in every sense of the word, mimicking the reading process. The emphasis is upon children experiencing the flow of the story and simultaneously seeing the written words that convey that story.

Have small book versions of your big books available for children to read on their own. Sometimes children may enjoy re-creating the text using the big book, but on other occasions they may like to have their own copy.

Display or store big books in the reading area. Following a shared reading session, the children will enjoy rereading the big book with some friends, or perhaps they will choose to reread the story on their own using the small book format.

2. Making a big book

Age range
Any age.

Group size
The whole class or small groups.

What you need
Good quality card appropriate for the intended book length, magazines, scissors, paper, felt-tipped pens, adhesive, appropriate binding such as staples, treasury tags or slide binders.

What to do
One of the main advantages of writing your own big book is that the children can be the main characters. Some of the most successful books have been those that the children have 'written' about themselves, such as the favourite food book where each child decides what he would like to eat and draws a self-portrait with the chosen food. In a similar way books about the school, the classroom or other familiar places enable the readers to bring knowledge to the text, which enables them to 'read' the text.

It is essential to decide on the text of the big book before beginning to make anything. The amount of text and the way the book will be illustrated will affect the number of pages and the size of the book. An eight-page book can be made from four sheets of good quality card, whereas a sixteen-page book made from card would be too bulky. It could, however, be made from paper held inside a more substantial cover.

Perhaps the most difficult part is to decide how to bind the book. The children will almost certainly want to be allowed to have the book on the floor, so the pages will need to turn easily and lie flat, but this can mean that they become detached from the spine!

With the children's help, plan out the format and text of the book and decide what text should go on to which page.

Remember that the print size should be sufficiently large for the group to see, and that too much text on a page can be very daunting.

Next, plan out the illustrations. Remember that each page should support or extend the text and should be sufficiently different from the previous page to maintain the reader's interest. Decide if you are going to include speech bubbles. If so, then the position of the speakers will have to be carefully chosen so that the first speaker's 'bubble' is towards the left hand side of the text and above that of the next speaker.

Divide off the amount of space required for text and roughly sketch in lines of text to establish that enough space

has been allocated. It is very easy to start lettering the text and then find there is no room for the last word!

Roughly plan the illustrations. This is especially important if speech bubbles are to be included. Discuss with the children any problems and encourage them to produce illustrations large enough for the group to see.

Write the text in the appropriate place and ask the children to provide the illustrations, either by cutting pictures from magazines or by making their own drawings. Stick the illustrations in place in the book.

Bind the book using any of the following methods:
• Have the book spiral bound. (Some teachers' centres and even some of the larger secondary schools may offer this facility.)
• Use a plastic slide binder to bind the books if there are not too many pages. However, this

does make turning the pages rather problematic.
• Using treasury tags enables the pages to lie flat on the floor but they do put a considerable strain on the holes made for them. Reinforcement and careful handling is required if the book is to last any time at all.
• Bind larger, heavier books between thin strips of wood and screw these together. However, again the pages tend not to lie flat on the floor.
• If the pages have been formed by folding a sheet of paper in half, it is possible to stitch the spine using a large back stitch and buttonhole thread.

Variations
• Put all the speech bubbles on to separate card and let the children decide who says what, then attach the bubbles to the appropriate speaker with Blu-Tack.
• For ESL pupils, write the speech bubbles in the language of the readers with a translation into English on the reverse.
• Write the continuous text on to strips of card and either ask

the children to fix it in place with Blu-Tack over existing text (so that they are matching text to text) or let them try to sequence the text with the pictures. In a similar way, make some of the illustrations detachable or provide extra detached illustrations which the children can place on to the pages.
• It is difficult for very young children to draw well enough to enable others to recognise the objects intended, so label drawings where necessary. However, sometimes patterns are all that is needed.
• Sometimes the young illustrator is unable to provide enough detail for the page to be interesting, in which case several artists can contribute. These 'multiple' offerings are often very successful.

3. Getting a discussion going

Age range
Any age.

Group size
Four to ten children.

What you need
A big book, an easel or bookstand, a pointer.

What to do
Before reading the book, show the children the cover of the book and read them the title, then ask them what they think the book is going to be about.

At an appropriate time, stop reading and ask the group what they think is going to happen next. Try to encourage the children to give reasons for their predictions and speculations.

After completing the reading session, ask the group if they could carry the story on. Ask them which characters they liked the best and which the least. Which was the funniest, the naughtiest or the kindest? Encourage them to justify their answers.

4. Turning it into drama

Age range
Any age.

Group size
The whole class, divided into small groups.

What you need
Puppets, craft materials, small props such as hats, masks, coats or shawls.

What to do
After a reading session, discuss with the class how many characters were in the story. Divide the class into sub-groups, and give each sub-group a character to discuss. Encourage the children to decide how the character would walk, talk, move and behave. At the end of five minutes, reassemble the whole class. Regroup the children so that each new group has every character represented, then ask the groups to prepare a small drama to perform to the rest of the class. At first the groups

will tend to re-enact the story they have heard, but with encouragement they may devise other dramas set round the same characters.

It is important for young readers to have the opportunity to role-play the characters in the books. Provide glove puppets, finger puppets, stick puppets or masks for the children to use for their role-play.

5. Scripted drama

Age range
Six to eight.

Group size
Twos or threes.

What you need
A variety of craft materials, garden cane, paper, scissors, pens, Blu-Tack.

What to do
Choose a story which has only two or three characters. Help the children to make large stick puppets to represent each of the characters.

Write out the dialogue for each character on to strips of paper and number the strips. Place the individual strips in speech order on to the back of the appropriate stick puppet, fixing them in place with Blu-Tack.

Let the children take a puppet each, then encourage them to read their parts holding the puppets in front of them.

CHAPTER 4

Developing a sight vocabulary

Many children arrive at school with a limited sight vocabulary. They may be able to recognise such things as:

• their name;
• their favourite cereal;
• their favourite television programme.

They can 'read' these in the same way as they can put two matching pictures together, but they are not looking in detail at the constituents of each word. If we were to offer them 'Tenage Mutent Her Turtes' written in the familiar typescript and using the appropriate colours, young children would be fooled into thinking that it was was written correctly and would believe it to say 'Teenage Mutant Hero Turtles'. Likewise, when offered their own name with only a minor variation (for example, Andrw), most children new to school would not notice the inaccuracy.

BACKGROUND

The evidence is that children newly arrived at school are absorbing generalisations about print but are not yet conscious of small differences, nor indeed are they aware of the significance of even minor alterations.

The factors determining a child's ability to recognise words depend upon two things:
• the motivation to know what the word says;
• the child's visual memory.
Both these factors need careful consideration when seeking to extend a child's sight vocabulary.

Flash cards

In the past children were taught a sight vocabulary through flash cards. Each card had an individual word written on it and the teacher sat with four or five children showing them the card and seeing who could recognise the words after they had been told them. One of the reasons why this approach to early reading remained so popular may have been that many children show a remarkable ability to recognise words after they have seen them only once or twice. Once the teacher was sure that the children recognised the words, the children could have the book which contained those words

(and, of course, earlier words acquired in similar flash card sessions).

Two things often occurred when the children met the practised words in the context of the book.
• Some children were unable to recognise the words in the book.
• Other children were able to say the words, but because the flash card practice had encouraged them to be *word readers* they ignored all other contextual clues. This word-by-word reading also interfered with children's ability to concentrate upon the meaning of what they were reading as they were so busy *remembering* what the words were.

It emerged that some children, who had been able to recognise the words on the flash cards but not in the book, had been setting up a complex pattern of associations

between the cards and the words they represented. For example, a child might have remembered the word 'play' because the ink was faded on that particular word or because there was a smudge in the left-hand corner of the card. Once denied these extraneous clues, the child would have no other means of identifying the words, and consequently often resorted to wild guessing.

A child who had stumbled on a particular word in a book would often hastily run through other words from the recently practised flash cards to see which one gained approval. This strategy, of course, pays no attention to the semantic relevance of the word. For example, a child might read the sentence, 'Dad sat on the big...' and then offer all the following words as possible endings to the sentence: happy/play/look/walk/chair. If the child had been encouraged to use semantic clues, he would probably have completed the sentence correctly.

Some schools extended the flash card approach by writing words on cards and putting them in tins for children to practise at home. Once a child had learned all the words she would be allowed to have the next book to read. However, this encourages children to think that if they found a word they did not know they must somehow be failing. Moreover, it offered no further strategies for decoding the unknown word.

In his book *Reading* (1978), Frank Smith quotes an experiment which revealed that a group of participants *instructed* to memorise words on cards remembered fewer of them than a group who had been asked not to memorise the words but to sort the cards into groups. In other words the latter group were expected to *think* about the words on the cards, to consider them on the basis of what they already knew and to make the words *meaningful*. This led Frank Smith to claim that comprehension takes care of memorisation. Giving children isolated words to recognise:
• does not make learning those words any easier;
• does not reflect the real demands reading makes upon the reader;
• gives no clue to the syntactic use of isolated words.

For example, there is a difference in meaning in the use of the word 'play' in the two sentences 'Let's play skipping' and 'We see a play'. Without a sense of syntax, children are deprived of many aids to understanding.

Contexts that make sense

The evidence is that isolated words are more difficult to recognise than words in context. Words learned and *then* put in context may be of

no advantage to the child who ignores contextual clues but strains to *remember* the word.

Let us return to the earlier example, 'Dad sat on the big...'. If a child has been encouraged to respond to the meaning of what is read, building up a picture of the likely missing word, then syntactically any of the following might be acceptable: bed/car/bath/chair, and so on. The child who offered these alternatives would at least be making sense of the sentence, unlike the earlier child who offered happy/play/look/walk.

Over-dependence on recognising decontextualised words, therefore, is not a reliable foundation for future reading success. Nevertheless, recognising *some* words by sight can give children an early

sense of what it is to be a reader. Quickly reading all of a simple book gives a child enormous encouragement. What is important is that the sight vocabulary should always be acquired in a context that makes sense.

For example, a teacher working with a group of four or five children might write a caption to a picture cut from a magazine, or write underneath a drawing, 'One day we went to a farm and we saw cows and hens'. After reading the caption several times with the children joining in, the teacher can start to draw the children's attention to closer details of the words by asking questions such as 'Which word says "farm"?' or 'Which word says "cows"?' Other questions can draw upon children's phonic knowledge. For example, 'What does this letter say?' or 'What does this word begin with?' Children could be guided towards

considering syntax and, for example, be encouraged to exchange 'cows' and 'hens' for 'goats' and 'sheep' but not for 'want' or 'help'.

This exercise differs from memorising flash cards because it requires retrieval and reconstruction from memory. It reminds children of the following important points.
• Reading is meaningful.
• We can remember some words because of the company they keep with other words.
• Picture clues might be helpful in reading.
• Our understanding of words is partially due to their syntactic use.

Of course, there are many occasions when we encourage children to recognise single words, but these occasions should reflect those they are likely to meet in life outside the classroom, for example, reading signs such as 'Enter', 'Closed', 'Exit', 'Telephone' and so on. For activities to encourage reading print in the environment see Chapter 2, pages 24 to 28.

1. My first book

Age range
Four to five.

Group size
Individuals.

What you need
Paper, adhesive tape, pencils, felt-tipped pens, card, scissors.

What to do
Fold the paper to make a very simple book.

Write a caption for the cover of the book, for example, 'Ben's book'. Ask the child to draw a picture of himself. Underneath the picture write 'Ben'. On subsequent pages write such captions as 'There is Mum' or 'Look at Ben playing football'.

On some pages, place a piece of thin card to cover the picture area, holding it in place with a strip of adhesive tape down one side. Write a question such as 'Is Mum here?' underneath the illustration space. Let the child choose whether to illustrate Mum or something else. The child can then share this page with others by asking the question and then lifting the card to reveal the answer.

Further activity
Once the children have completed their books and read them several times, make cards of the words used in the books and show the children how to match the cards to the words in their own book. Place each card below the word in the child's book so that they make the connection between the words they handle and the words they can 'read' in their own book.

2. Match-a-sentence

Age range
Five to six.

Group size
Threes or fours.

What you need
Card, scissors, felt-tipped pens.

What to do
This game encourages children to reread their sentences, and

at the same time it places all sight vocabulary in a meaningful context.

Before the activity, devise a set of sentences using the vocabulary that the children have encountered in stories or in other language work in the classroom. Write the sentences on to card, then write each individual word from the sentences on to separate pieces of card. For example, if you write the sentence 'Mog got in her spaceship' you will need individual cards for the words 'Mog', 'got' etc.
Ask the children to sit round tables in small groups. Let each child take a sentence strip and place it in front of herself. Check that each child can read her sentence and give support where necessary.

Place the cards with individual words face down in the centre of the table. Let each child take it in turn to pick a card and to check whether it matches a word in her sentence strip. If it matches, let the child place it above the corresponding word; if it does not match, ask the child to return it to the table. The winner is the first player to match all the words in her sentence.

3. Labels

Age range
Five to six.

Group size
Five or six children.

What you need
Card, pen.

What to do
Cut some pieces of card into strips measuring 18cm by 6cm.

On each piece of card, write the name of an object in the classroom, such as table, chair, box, book and basin.

Fan out the cards, then let the children take it in turn to choose one. Ask the children to place the cards in the correct position in the classroom.

When all the cards have been positioned, send the children in turn to retrieve them. Ask them to read out the card before handing it over to be put back in the pile.

4. Look alike

Age range
Five to six.

Group size
Two to four children.

What you need
Card, scissors, copies of photocopiable pages 166 and 167, felt-tipped pens.

What to do
Choose six words which can be easily illustrated, such as house, book and so on. (These can be linked with the vocabulary of a popular book or series of books, such as the

Meg and Mog series.) Make two sets of six cards with pictures illustrating the chosen words. On another 12 cards write the corresponding words. Photocopiable pages 166 and 167 give some sample cards.

Place the 12 picture cards face down on the table and ask the children to take it in turns to select and name any two cards. If the cards match, let the child keep the pair and have another go. When the child fails to select a matching pair, the cards should be turned back and the next child allowed a turn. Continue play in this way until all cards have been successfully matched.

When the children are sufficiently confident, repeat the game using only the word cards. Encourage the children to say the words as they turn over the cards.

Follow this by selecting six different picture cards and the six corresponding word cards and asking the children to play as before. Explain that the players must now name the picture and say the word before keeping the pair.

Variation
For older or more able children, play as above but add in six extra matching word and picture combinations.

5. Happy families

Age range
Six to seven.

Group size
Three or four children.

What you need
Card, scissors, felt-tipped pens, a 'sentence-maker' stand.

What to do
Make 20 cards and label them so that you have five 'families', each containing four things.

For example:
• Colours: red, blue, green, yellow;
• Animals: dog, cat, rabbit, mouse;
• School: classroom, hall, kitchen, office;
• Music: drum, bell, piano, triangle;
• Street: bus, car, lorry, bike.
  Write one of the words on each of the cards. Use a symbol to identify each family.

Ensure that the children familiarise themselves with the words and the sets to which

they belong before they start the game.

Deal out all the cards. (Some children may find it easier to handle the cards if they are allowed to stand them up in a 'sentence-maker' stand.) Let the players take it in turn to ask the other children for the missing cards of a 'family', for example, 'Please have you got the colour blue?' If the other person has the card it must be handed over. Let the child continue asking round the group until the answer is, 'Sorry, I have not got...'. Then let the player who could not provide the card have a turn to ask the others. Play finishes when all the sets have been collected. The winner is the player with the most sets.

Variation

For younger children, make 24 cards with nouns only, with the word written on one side and a picture of the object on the other.

Place the cards word side up for each player to read. Once a player has 'read' a word, he can turn the card over to check that what he has said matches the picture. This self-checking system can be very useful in the busy classroom when it may not be possible for an adult to be on hand to supervise the game.

6. Space race game

Age range
Six to seven.

Group size
Three or four children.

What you need
Copies of photocopiable page 168, card, scissors, felt-tipped pens, die, counters, small toys.

What to do
This game allows for self-checking. Many children can match word-to-word before they can 'read', and this gives them the confidence to examine each word carefully.

Using photocopiable page 168, make a baseboard track for each group of children. Write a word in every third square of the track and write the same words on small pieces of card and put them in the centre of the board.

Ensure that all players of this game sit so that they can see the words in the centre of the board the right way up. Give each child a counter and put a pile of small toys beside the board.

Let the children take turns to throw the die and move counters around the board. When a child lands on a square with a word, ask him to scan the words in the centre to find the matching word. If he can match the words, let him take a toy from the pile. The winner is the player with most toys.

7. Word race

Age range
Six to seven.

Group size
Three to four children.

What you need
Copies of photocopiable page 169, a die, counters, card, a felt-tipped pen, scissors.

What to do
Before the activity, make a baseboard track using photocopiable page 169. Make 30 small cards, each with a word written on it.

Place the 30 cards in a stack, face down on the table. Give each child a counter and ask them to place their counters by the start. Let each player take it in turn to throw the die and turn over a card. Explain that the player can only move her counter along the number of squares shown on the die if she can say the word on the card she draws. If she cannot say the word she misses her turn.

The next child who throws the die can then opt either to say the first child's word before moving the counter the number shown on the die, or select the next card from the pile.

Explain that when a child reaches the end of the track, if for example she throws a five but needs only three to finish, she may only move one space forward (provided she reads the word correctly). This makes for a more exciting ending.

CHAPTER 5

Phonics

If there is any area of teaching reading that is likely to evoke strong feelings and a wide diversity of opinion, it is that of phonics. Arguments rage over when, how much, in what order and with what material young readers should be introduced to letter sounds. An enormous amount of research and effort has been put into trying to decide the answers to these questions.

During the late 1970s and 1980s, teaching phonics fell into disrepute, not because teachers felt that knowledge of letter sounds was of no value, but rather because the published material which was firmly based on a 'phonic' approach to reading frequently made little sense and read more like a tongue-twister than a piece of informative or interesting text.

'Pat hugs Rag Bag.
Fat, red Rag Bag.
And sad is Nat,
the big fat cat.

Nat tugs Rag Bag
in the mud.
Mum has Rag Bag.
Sad, red Rag Bag.'
(Morris, 1974.)

In spite of this, virtually all schools, according to the HMI report *Standards of Reading in the United Kingdom (DES 1990b)*, appear to have attempted to teach some phonic awareness. The differences between schools seem to be mostly a matter of emphasis.

BACKGROUND

Phonics, phonetics and phonemes

Before trying to establish what research can tell us about the teaching of phonics, it is necessary to define what is meant by the different terms. In many articles and books, the terms 'phonics' and 'phonetics' appear to be synonymous. However, the dictionary suggests that *phonics* is 'the method which is used when teaching students to associate letters with their phonetic values' (*Collins English Dictionary*).

A *phoneme* describes a speech sound in any language that serves to distinguish one word from another. For example, in English the letters 'b' and 'p' are separate phonemes as they help us to recognise the difference between 'bet' and 'pet', and 'a' and 'i' are phonemes when they help us to distinguish between 'at' and 'it'. However, the two 'l's in 'little' are not separate phonemes as they can be transposed without any change of meaning. For the purposes of this chapter, the teaching of 'phonics' is taken to mean the way in which children learn to associate a letter with a sound.

Research and the pre-school child

For a detailed summary of research in this field, see Adams, 1990.

In 1967, J. Chall astounded many teachers by stating that knowledge of the alphabet by pre-readers was a strong predictor of early reading achievement. This was found to be the single 'best predictor of first year reading achievement, closely followed by an ability to distinguish between phonemes' (Bond and Dystra 1967). As a result, numerous parents taught their pre-school children the alphabet. Unfortunately, this did not achieve the desired results, and a closer examination of the research was undertaken. It was suggested that those children who came to school knowing the alphabet were more likely to come from homes where reading was given a high profile. Another suggestion was that knowledge of the alphabet was itself evidence that the children had the necessary memory skills and attention span that would ensure later success. Finally, researchers concluded that just knowing the alphabet did not help much. The genuine predictor was the speed and ease with which children could identify and name the letters. It was familiarity with the letters and the ability to pay attention to the fine differences between the letters that ensured success.

It was argued that children who automatically saw the letters as 'wholes' were also those children who saw words as patterns of letters and saw the essential differences between words. These children quickly acquired a visual vocabulary.

Coupled with this was the suggestion that many letter

names are related to their sounds, so that by knowing the name the child was more likely to be able to attach the appropriate sound to that letter (for example, this is a 'B' and its sound is /b/, or this is a 'T' and the sound is /t/).

More recently researchers have shown that many pre-school children have begun to master the alphabetic principles before they have been formally taught. As 'emergent' writing becomes more widespread in reception classes, so this knowledge becomes more easily recognised. A 'rising five' child asked her teacher to write for her the sentence, 'This is my class and it's full of children'. The teacher suggested that first she should do her best to write what she could. The child wrote 'T si m c and its F of C'. Her knowledge of the alphabetic system for both letter names and sounds was considerable.

Pre-school research seems to have established that letter-naming is something that most young children can acquire and that this knowledge is valuable

for early reading. The researchers stress the need for early, systematic instruction with emphasis upon letter names, shapes and sounds.

Should phonic instruction be delayed?

Many teachers have been persuaded that attention to letter sounds is better delayed until the child is around seven years of age. This idea seems to have been based upon two factors.

Firstly, it is thought that many young children find it difficult to hear the differences between letters before they are seven. Indeed, Kevin Murphy of the audiology department in the Royal Berkshire Hospital has suggested that one in three children suffer considerable hearing loss during their first two years in school as at this time they are very susceptible to colds and infections. By seven years of age most

children do seem to be able to separate the sounds more easily. However, it is very difficult to establish whether this is actually due to improved hearing, or whether they only appear to separate the sounds because they now have a good visual image of the word.

Secondly, it was thought that children need a mental age of seven in order to be ready to 'use' sounds. This was based on research undertaken in 1937 by Dolch and Bloomster. The enormous amount of more recent research into children's emergent writing would indicate that young children are, in fact, using both letter names and sounds much earlier than this. It is only since very young children have been encouraged to write without teacher support that

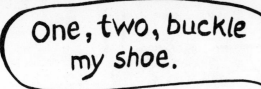

the extent to which they are using a letter and sound match has become known. In 1985, Yopp and Singer disproved the claim that a mental age of seven was needed before children should be introduced to sounds. They argued that 'the role of mental age is not one of limiting what a child can learn but of limiting the ways in which they can be effectively taught'.

Conclusion

• There is no specific age at which children should be introduced to letter and sound matching.
• It is essential for the teacher to discover what the individual child knows and to build from that.
• All children need to receive careful, systematic and relevant teaching of phonics at some stage, but they need guidance as to when to use this strategy.

The child who cannot 'hear' letter sounds

The research of Bryant and Bradley (1985) showed that children as young as three, who were introduced to rhyme

and developed an ear for these sounds, made better progress with early reading. They also showed that attention and sensitivity to rhyme and rhythm could easily be developed in pre-school children.

In 1990, Goswami and Bryant continued this work with young children who were beginning to read. They found that children were able to separate words into sound 'chunks' but were not able to separate individual letters.

They showed that children were able to identify the initial 'sound' (the 'onset') from the next 'sound' (the 'rime'). For example, they could separate /c/ from /at/, (/c/ being the onset, and /at/ being the rime) or could separate /k/ (the onset) from /ing/ (the rime). However, it was very difficult for children to identify individual phonemes, such as the /a/ in cat. This sound is acoustically evanescent, that is, it has no boundaries as a sound because it is so closely attached to the /t/.

This work seems to imply that children recognise phonemes more easily when they form the onset of a word, and that they need to be encouraged to identify the rimes that follow, not as individual letters but as a string. Obviously this is more

easily done with rhyming rimes.

Children who can recognise rhyme demonstrate that they can categorise words on the basis of their sounds. Goswami and Bryant concluded, though, that there was no evidence that children who were learning to read relied strongly on letter/sound relationships to help them read words, but that there was strong evidence that they did use these relationships when writing.

However, in a research project undertaken in Cumbria in 1991, Peter Hatcher monitored the reading progress of four different groups of poor readers aged seven. One group was given phonic teaching as an isolated skill, one group had phonic teaching linked to reading, one group concentrated on reading alone and the last group were the control. The group that had phonics linked to reading made significant gains over the others. The results showed the effectiveness of a structured reading procedure that united the teaching of phonics to reading. The researchers felt their findings provided strong support for the idea that good phonological skills and reading are causally related.

Teaching letter sounds

Is there such a thing as a 'best' order in which to teach letter sounds?

The quick answer to this is 'no'. What all researchers stress is that phonic teaching must be kept in a meaningful context and that learning to read has to rely upon a desire for comprehension. Teaching phonics in isolation generally negates the search for comprehension. Too many of our poorest readers decode the sounds but make no sense of the text. They have come to believe that teachers want them to make the correct sounds to the letters and, having produced them, assume that this is the final goal. They fail to go on to seek for the meaning in the words.

Different children will come to school knowing very different sounds and symbols. They will probably know the initial letter of their names, and perhaps some of the different letters taken from signs near their homes. This knowledge is the obvious starting point for letter recognition and ensures that children are building upon letters that are important to them. However, as children's sight vocabulary grows, it is possible to use this to help them link sounds and symbols. The child can reinforce this growing knowledge through such activities as sharing alphabet books, matching individual letters, playing with plastic or wooden alphabets, finding pictures of objects that have the same onsets, and so on.

Some teachers have found it useful to teach children letters in order of writing frequency, while others like to cluster them according to how the sound is produced, for example, with the lips, with the tongue on the roof of the mouth and so on. So long as the teacher is consistent and confident, letter order is a matter of individual choice.

What about the confusable letters?
Many children confuse 'mirror image' letters (for example, b and d; p and q; u and n) and, although they know letter sounds, they cannot regularly attach the right sound to the letter shape. Nearly all the researchers suggest that as far as possible these letters should be kept well apart. The feeling is that the child should become familiar with one letter before being presented with its mirror image. Williams and Ackerman (1971) found there was quicker assimilation if confusable letters were kept apart. However, this is not to say that the teacher should go to great lengths to offer sentences that do not contain a 'b' and a 'd'. It is rather a question of choosing one of the letters to highlight and perhaps practise in 'handwriting' before the other.

Some popular phonic material has endeavoured to help children attach sounds to letters by anthropomorphising the letters. Many children delight in the stories that are

told about the letters, and television has been quick to provide animated cartoons along the same lines. For some children these are a valuable and helpful aid. However, other children seem to be unable to detach the sound of the letter from its personalised name. When they look at the letter in a book they 'see' the character rather than the sound and this can lead to a slow and painful reading of the text. Again, this approach has been shown to be of much greater value for children learning to write than for learning to read.

Conclusion
• Keep mirror image letters apart when specifically teaching a letter shape and sound.
• Use handwriting practice to reinforce letter shape and sound.

Keeping a record

Keeping a careful record of what a child can do is essential in today's busy classroom. The easiest way to ascertain which letters a child already knows on entry to school is to ask him to write for you without giving him direct support (emergent writing). When you then ask him what he has written, it is comparatively easy to see if he knows letter shapes, and whether he can match some letters and sounds or even letter names.

The child who wrote 'T si m c and its F of C' shows us that she knows that when you write you leave spaces between words. She also knows the boundaries of these words. (Many children find separating 'the' from its noun very difficult. They think of it as 'thetable' and, therefore, one word.) She also knows of at least eight letter and sound matches and, as she turned to the teacher and asked 'Does class begin with a C or a K?', she obviously knows the difference between these letter names and that they carry similar sounds.

When sharing writing and reading with children, it should be possible to keep a record of the letter names, sounds, blends, diagraphs and lower case/upper case recognition that the child knows. As this record of achievement progresses, it is valuable with some children to show them the record and discuss with them the few 'unusual' bits that they still have to learn. Far too often a child does not know the goal to which he is working, and it is hardly surprising that he then fails to reach it.

ACTIVITIES

1. Recording phonic knowledge

Age range
Any age.

Group size
Individuals.

What you need
Copies of photocopiable pages 170 and 171.

What to do
Over the course of a few days, as you observe the children in the classroom, use copies of photocopiable page 170 to record their phonic knowledge.

Photocopiable page 171 gives a simple letter/sound recording sheet. These sheets can also be used as a record for the rest of the activities in this chapter.

2. Rhyme race

Age range
Five to seven.

Group size
Two or three children.

What you need
A copy of photocopiable page 172, small coloured adhesive paper circles, a die, counters.

What to do
Before the activity, make copies of photocopiable page 172 and colour the circles in sequence, red, blue, green, yellow. Stick six coloured circles on the sides of the die, one red, one blue, one green, one yellow and two white.

Let one child roll the die and place his counter on the colour shown. Ask him to say a word that rhymes with the picture in that circle. If he is successful, allow him to move forward to the next circle as a reward before the next child has a turn. If he is unsuccessful, ask him to remain on the same circle until his next turn, when he may throw the dice again and move the appropriate number of squares. Let the other players take it in turns to

throw the die, move and attempt to rhyme in the same way. The first player to finish wins.

3. Alpha-track

Age range
Five to seven.

Group size
Individuals.

What you need
Copies of photocopiable pages 173 and 174, pencils.

What to do
Distribute copies of photocopiable pages 173 and 174. Ask the children to work through the game boards, trying to find all the letters of the alphabet in order.

4. First out

Age range
Five to seven.

Group size
Two or three children.

What you need
Cardboard, felt-tipped pen, scissors, clear adhesive film.

What to do
This activity helps children to gain familiarity with alphabet order. This is essential if they are to become confident and efficient users of reference books.

Before the activity, make a set of alphabet cards, either lower case or upper case, so that each group can have a set. Mount the letters on card and cover them with clear adhesive film.

Deal out all the cards, with one hand for each player in the group, plus a 'blind' hand. Ask the players to look at their cards. For easy viewing, the children may prefer to lay their cards out in front of them.

Explain to the children that they are going to try to make an alphabet sequence. Ask the child with the 'M' card to start the game by placing this card face up on the table. Explain that the player to the left of the first child should now have a turn. Ask her whether she can place a correct card to either side of the letter 'M'. Allow her to continue until she is unable to put any more letters in the correct place.

Continue the game with children taking it in turn to add a letter to one or other end of the growing alphabet sequence.

If a child cannot go, ask him to take a card from the 'blind' hand and, if possible, add this to the alphabet line. If the card cannot be used, ask the child to put one of his cards to the bottom of the 'blind' hand.

The first player to get rid of all his cards is the winner.

Variations
• Before dealing, ask the children to suggest a different starting letter. By altering the starting point in this way, children are helped to become familiar with alphabet order without constantly having to return to the letter 'a' to get their bearings when saying or sequencing the alphabet.
• Combine a set of upper and lower case cards and sequence two alphabets in tandem. This could be either one upper case and one lower case or two mixed alphabets. You may need to increase the number of players for this variation.
• For children who are only just learning their alphabet, or who are uncertain of the alphabet, try using just one half of the alphabet.

5. Initial ideas

Age range
Five to eight.

Group size
The whole class or small groups.

What you need
No special equipment.

What to do
Name an object in the classroom or say a word starting with a particular letter. Invite the children to say another word beginning with the same sound. Let the first child to offer a correct phonic match continue the game, by saying another word starting with the same sound and asking one of the group to supply yet another word starting with the same sound. Continue the game in this way until no more initial ideas for that sound can be thought of.

Variations
• This activity can be varied by changing the initial sound after every three or four 'matched' words.
• Extend the game by saying a word and saying the name of the letter with which it starts, then inviting the children to say another word beginning

with the same letter. For example, if you say, 'Apple begins with "A". What else do you know that starts with "A"?', the first child to offer a correct alphabetic match, such as 'Andrew begins with "A"', continues the game. Continue around the group as in the original game. If a child offers a word without naming the initial letter, allow the next child to have the next turn.

6. Alphabet zoo

Age range
Five to seven.

Group size
The whole class or small groups.

What you need
No special equipment.

What to do
Start an alphabet sequence story by saying, for example, 'I went to the zoo and I saw some apes', then passing the sequence on to one of the children. Ask the child to repeat the first sentence and add another animal or animal group using the next letter of the alphabet, for example 'I went to the zoo and I saw some apes and some bears'. Pass the sequence on for four, five or six letters and then start another story and another sequence, beginning with a different letter of the alphabet.

This activity helps children develop the ability to say any sequence of letters without having to return to 'A' each time they want to remember what precedes or follows a particular letter – a much-needed skill when using reference books.

7. Alphabet collage

Age range
Five to seven.

Group size
The whole class or small groups.

What you need
Frieze paper, board, collage materials, felt-tipped pens, scissors, adhesive.

What to do
Write the letters of the alphabet on the board and encourage the children to tell you the names and sounds of the letters. Cover part of the classroom wall with plain frieze paper, making sure it is at the children's height. Discuss the possibility of making an alphabet collage. Suggest that they might like to try to include something to represent each letter of the alphabet in their collage.

Allocate a letter to each child or group of children. Ask them to choose an object which begins with their allocated letter. After discussion, allow some time for the children to report back to the whole class. This 'talk back' can prove very helpful as children will often offer additional suggestions to each other with the result that nobody is left feeling that the task is too difficult for them.

Finally let the children make the collage using a range of materials. Label each object with the appropriate letter so that it can be used as a reference or reminder. This activity can be varied by having a thematic focus, such as 'Animals' or 'Food'.

CHAPTER 6

Organising & displaying reading resources

If children are to become independent readers, it is important that they have access to a range of reading material which, as far as possible, reflects the 'real world'. That is to say, classroom resources should include comics, magazines, catalogues, dictionaries, newspapers, fiction, non-fiction and reference books. In this way, children will be able to read from a wide variety of texts according to their interest, inclination or need. The way in which reading resources are organised is an important consideration in trying to develop children's reading interests and abilities.

Who does the organising?

Traditionally, educational publishers who produced graded reading schemes provided an organisational principle ready-made for the teacher. Because it was believed that reading was dependent on slowly accumulating either a sight vocabulary or a range of phonic skills, children were obliged to work their way through these books in a strictly controlled order. Often it was assumed that children would only be able to read these books if they could recognise the separate words first. Between books the child was given the new vocabulary to learn for the next book. Each time, children had to demonstrate that they could recognise these new words; then they were allowed the book!

Many educational publishers listed the new vocabulary inside the back cover. This invited teachers to test the words out of context when the child had read the book. It was not unknown for children to fail this second test and to have to reread the book, only to be tested again on the word list at the back. In the research reported in Southgate et al (1976), one little girl had been on one book for a year!

In reaction to the control exerted by the single scheme system, many teachers began to reconsider how reading resources could be organised.

Colour-coding resources

In order to provide a wider range of material and to help children move away from the pre-programmed approach to reading, teachers began to combine books from several series into broad levels which they colour-coded. Children were encouraged to select a book from within a colour. This meant that they had more chance of choosing a book they could read but that also reflected their interests. This supported freedom has helped children to develop the ability to choose or reject books.

How to colour-code books

Colour-coding is not associated with a specific reading age but rather with the development of a growth in reading matched to a child's interest and ability.

Some schools take just one reading scheme as a basis for coding and use the stages as

markers for each level, supplemented with books from other sources. Criteria for coding include sentence length, sentence complexity, the amount of text on a page, the match between the vocabulary of the scheme and the books that are added to each level and the match between pictures and text.

Other schools do not emphasise one scheme above the rest but provide colour-coded levels, using similar criteria. Initial judgements about the level of the books are tested by trying out books with groups of children before the books are finally coded.

Some schools, however, have become concerned about the competition among both parents and children that the colour-coding can lead to. They feel that a more realistic introduction to the world of books can be provided without the external symbol of colours. This requires an extensive knowledge about the books in the classroom on the part of the teacher. In these schools the teacher and the child select books together, or the teacher may recommend certain titles that she considers are within the capabilities and interest of the child.

Generally teachers have tended not to use colour-coding for non-fiction as there has not been much simple non-fiction available. As this area expands, the possibility of coding may arise. However, the knowledge and interest the reader brings to non-fiction texts can dramatically affect their ability to read a text. This has been called the 'pterodactyl syndrome', as the child who is enthusiastic and knowledgeable about these creatures can often read texts that might appear to be far too difficult.

Organising early readers

The following points about organisation need to be addressed by the whole staff before drawing up a reading policy. There is no obvious right or wrong way to organise early reading books; in many cases, the physical building or the amount of resources available may finally influence the decision, but teachers who have considered all the possibilities and come to a corporate decision are much more likely to help children to become readers. Consider the following questions when discussing grading:

• Does grading help to organise the resources more effectively?
• What impression of reading do children get from this method of organisation?
• What impression of reading do parents get from this method of organisation?
• Does the organisation of the books enable children to learn how to choose?
• Is grading purely a device to keep the books in a particular order?
• Does grading foster a competitive attitude towards reading?

The following analysis may help to answer these questions.

Strengths

• Careful grading of books can help some children select from an appropriate range or level.
• It prevents children from taking home books that parents may feel are too difficult.
• It can provide a structure for the inexperienced teacher.
• It may build up children's confidence, since when books are ungraded the quantity of unfamiliar books may be daunting to the very young reader.
• Grading books helps teachers to direct children's choices.

Faced with a totally free choice children may choose the same book time after time, not because it is a favourite but because they lack the confidence to choose anything new.
• Grading makes parents feel they understand the system. When books are not graded, parents may become anxious, feeling that there is no obvious structure to the reading system.
• Grading ensures that children know where to put the books back.

Weaknesses

• Grading books can promote an over-emphasis on 'getting on' rather than reading for meaning.
• It can result in children perceiving reading as a hierarchical process.
• It entails a danger that children will think of books

only in terms of their 'colour sticker' rather than in terms of title, author and content. They may also see books in terms of 'reading books' and 'other books'.
• Grading may not help children to learn how to select books.
• It may not provide sufficient titles to allow children to select according to their interest, need or inclination. An ungraded system is more likely to provide a choice of fiction or non-fiction.
• Grading is unlikely to encourage discussion with the teacher about why the child has chosen a particular book.
• It provides little encouragement to reread favourite books.
• Grading might make parents anxious about their child's progress through the levels, and in turn lead to pressure on the child.

Consideration of the points made above has led many teachers to abandon an obviously graded approach. They have used their own knowledge of the books in their classroom to help children to select appropriately. This system recognises the relationship between the reader and the text that allows the child to become an active reader.

Can the two systems work together?

Some schools follow a single graded system for hearing children read and monitoring their progress. This is extended by supplementing the scheme with a wide variety of broadly graded selected books. It is from this section that the children can choose those books they want to take home or read in school for themselves. However, this form of organisation offers the children conflicting messages. They, and their parents, see the 'scheme' book as the important one and the rest as inferior. Some children actually split the reading activity into the *important one*, which takes place when they read to the teacher from their 'reading book', and the *other one* which

they see as 'passing time'. This dangerous split can all too often mean that children learn some of the mechanics of reading but they may not turn to books for enjoyment or information. This process can also mean that the 'reading book' is only read to an adult in the classroom two or three times a week. The child only reads short extracts of print and often forgets the previous events in the book. Thus she gets a fragmented reading experience, loses the thread of the story and cannot respond to the text, while believing that this is the reading of greatest importance.

Teachers have argued that by dividing books in this way they have avoided parents drilling children in the vocabulary of the reading scheme in order to hurry the child on to the next book. They have sent home the 'enjoyable

read' so that the parent sits and cuddles the child and doesn't worry over the odd reading error, and kept away the text that the child must 'tackle'. All too often, rather than reducing parental worry, this approach has increased it – even to the extent that parents have then bought the complete scheme for use at home and tested the child on it! This action undermines the carefully considered organisation of the school. Parents feel that they must be helping by reinforcing the vocabulary of the 'school reading book'. This good intention can have harmful

consequences for young readers, as it is all too easy for them to 'fail' in front of their parents and both they and their parents may begin to think the child is a 'poor' reader. Believing you are not good at something is the quickest way to failure.

This form of organisation offers a double standard to children who are learning to read. It encourages a belief that reading in school and reading outside school are two different activities, one of which is much more important than the other. It is a pitfall that must be considered when discussing reading organisation.

Displaying books

Obviously how the books are displayed in a school will depend to a large extent upon the number of books, the classes that need access to them and the layout of the building. However, the major consideration should be to ensure that all children have reasonably quick and easy access to the books. Most teachers of young children prefer a class 'book corner'.

Organising the book corner

Try to provide as many of the following as possible:
• a carpeted area;
• comfortable seating, such as floor cushions, bean bags, small tables and chairs;
• low shelving that allows the children to see the front covers of as many books as possible (wire racks may save space but they are difficult for children to use);
• low trolleys or book boxes to entice children to browse;
• a tape recorder and headphones for using with story tapes;
• a large teddy to read to (many children have happily shared their books with such a character).

Choosing books

General criteria

The following criteria may be applied when choosing books for the book corner.
• Look for language that is memorable and that does not seem contrived or unnatural.
• Choose texts that promote reflection or discussion, and to which the reader will want to return.
• Choose texts that are non-racist and do not demean people from any nationality, race or creed.

• Look for texts that discourage role stereotyping, but not to the point of detracting from the integrity of the book.
• Include some dual-language texts of quality stories and non-fiction.
• Include books that come to terms with emotions such as fear and anger.
• Choose books that extend a child's knowledge of the world, self and others.
• Select books that have reasonable print size, colour and style.

Ensuring variety

The following are some more specific suggestions for ensuring a variety of books.
• Include good quality fiction for all pupils, whatever their level of reading.
• Choose a range of good quality non-fiction, using both photographic and drawn illustrations.
• Select different texts offering a wide variety of reads, such as poetry, riddles, folk tales, plays, jokes, comics, adventure stories and biographies.

• Have available a wide variety of good illustrations, from cartoon drawings to oil paintings.
• Include a wide variety of wordless books, pop-up books and picture books for children of all ages.

Finally, consider buying a minimum of 100 books per class. The range of books should include new books, old books, thick books, thin books, large books, small books and books that have been written by the children. Remember that your enthusiasm for books can be made apparent by:
• discussing books with children;
• making books important;
• displaying books attractively;
• reading small sections of the book to whet the potential reader's appetite;
• being seen to read for pleasure yourself.

To encourage children to become familiar with all the books, let two or three children per week be responsible for the display and the general upkeep of the books.

Acquiring other reading resources

As experienced readers, we read on many levels. For example, there are times when we want a light read and choose a magazine or short

story, and others when we read to acquire information. Young readers share this need to read for different reasons and the classroom resources should take account of this. A collection including comics, hobby magazines, maps and catalogues will supplement the classroom book provision and reflect the range of reading material that children see outside school. Many children and their families buy various magazines and comics. Explain to parents and children your reasons for extending reading provision in your school and ask them to donate any reading materials that are unwanted.

Ask the children to draw up a rota for care and maintenance of these resources, and to develop a list of criteria for inclusion or exclusion in the collection of materials. For example:
• Is the comic or magazine too old and too out of date?
• Is it too scruffy and dog-eared?
• Are any pages missing?
• Is there anybody in the class who is interested in the subject?

Management and display

When developing these resources it is important to consider how they will be managed and whether there should be any specific time for reading them.

Magazines and comics should be stored tidily in boxes or racks. They are notoriously difficult to keep looking attractive, as anyone who has been in the doctor's or dentist's waiting room will know. This means that they need to be constantly discarded and replaced.

Promoting books

One idea that has promoted real knowledge of the resources in the classroom is to suggest a theme or topic on which the children can mount an appropriate display of books. Small children are quite capable of selecting the books, although they may not always display them to your standard. They frequently put 'the biggest and best' at the front! Given time and opportunity, however, they will become adept at managing their own resources.

ACTIVITIES

1. Character posters

Age range
Any age.

Group size
Two to four children.

What you need
Large pieces of paper, felt-tipped pens.

What to do
Choose a book you have shared with a group of children, then ask them to make posters illustrating the characters. Ask them to write down their favourite characters or make a list of other features such as places, food or people, etc found in the book.

Display the posters in the book corner.

2. Question posters

Age range
Any age.

Group size
The whole class.

What you need
Large sheets of paper, felt-tipped pens, a favourite book, display materials.

What to do
Choose a book you are going to read aloud, or one that many children have already read.

Write out ten simple questions on a large sheet of paper. Let the children try to answer all the questions. Sometimes it can be valuable to let the children try to think up questions.

Help the children to devise an illustrated display of question posters to place around the relevant book. Ask them to think of relevant artefacts for their display (for

example, wellington boots and marmalade sandwiches for books about Paddington).

3. Quiz posters

Age range
Any age.

Group size
A minimum of four children.

What you need
Large sheets of paper, books on a specific topic.

What to do
Choose a topic about which you have plenty of books in the classroom. Discuss the topic generally in class, then let the children think up a variety of questions. Write down the questions on a large sheet of paper.

With the children's help, sort out the questions into groups. For example, if the topic is about frogs, questions could be sorted as follows:
• questions about the life cycle of the frog;
• questions about the habits of the adult frog;
• questions about the habitat of the frog.

Ask the children to see if they can find out the answers from any of the books you have provided. Let the children write down against the question the name of the book and the page on which they found the answers.

4. A class wall frieze

Age range
Any age.

Group size
The whole class.

What you need
Paper, frieze paper, paints, pencils, crayons, a favourite book.

What to do
Talk about a book you have shared with the children.

Let the children work out a picture sequence which illustrates the plot, so that

each child is allocated a particular event in the book. Encourage the children to illustrate their event, then mount the pictures in sequence as a frieze round the wall.

5. 'Top of the pops'

Age range
Any age.

Group size
The whole class.

What you need
Ten books, a large sheet of paper, ten strips of paper with a book title written on each, card, scissors, Blu-Tack, felt-tipped pens.

What to do
Choose ten books from the book corner.

Using Blu-Tack, fix the title strips down the left hand side of a large piece of paper. Cut out a number of circles from card and draw smiling and frowning faces on them.

Let the children read the books, then, depending on whether or not they liked the book, ask them to fix a smiling or frowning face beside the title of the book with Blu-Tack.

After half a term, ask the children to check which book has the most smiles. Let them rearrange the book titles on the chart in order of merit.

6. Story word squares

Age range
Any age.

Group size
Individuals or pairs.

What you need
Copies of photocopiable page 175, a supply of books, pencils.

What to do

Distribute copies of photocopiable page 175. Ask each child to choose a book and write its title on the back of the photocopiable sheet.

Ask the children to list the characters and places in the story on the back of the sheet, then check the spelling of these words. When they are satisfied with the spelling, let them place the chosen words on to the grid like a word-search puzzle, filling the remaining spaces with random letters.

When they have filled the grid, let children who have read the same book swap sheets. Ask the children to do a 'word search' to try to find all the words that are hidden in the grid. When the children think they have found all the words, let them check their lists against the answers on the back of the sheet.

7. Thematic week

Age range
Any age.

Group size
The whole class.

What you need
An accessible display space, thematically related books and toys.

What to do
Ask the children to bring in toys and books relating to a particular theme, such as:
• things that move;
• weather and seasons;
• teddy bears;
• grandparents.

Let the children arrange the display and label it. Invite other classes to come and visit the display.

Read to the class as many stories and poems related to the theme as possible. Visiting classes, parents and governors could be invited to share stories.

CHAPTER 7

Hearing children read

Many teachers consider hearing children read the 'single most important component of good practice' (Gray, 1979). Certainly most parents consider that the time their child spends sharing a book with a teacher is very important, and it is recognised that this time must be used to the best advantage.

Traditionally, teachers were expected to hear every child in their class read to them every day. Stories abound of teachers spending every available minute trying to fit in a daily 'reading time' for classes of 40-plus infants, as headteachers were notorious for checking that every child had been 'heard'. In order to do this, the 'two lines' read came into existence, as that was all there was time to hear.

BACKGROUND

Supporting reading

It will not surprise you to learn that this practice was not the most effective way of supporting children's reading. The Extending Beginning Reading project (Southgate et al. 1976) disclosed that hearing individual children for longer periods of time enabled the teacher to diagnose the reader's strengths and weaknesses. Using this knowledge, the teacher was then able to help the child to choose a suitable book. Furthermore, it was soon realised that talking about the book and then hearing the child read for several minutes gave the teacher far greater insights, which in turn led to more effective teaching.

The habit of hearing reading for longer periods meant that it was impossible for the teacher to hear every child in the class individually every day. It is now more common practice for a very young reader to be with the teacher two or three times a week.

Of course, this is not the only time a teacher hears a child read. On numerous occasions, the teacher and the child are reading to each other; reading notices, reading words on the wall displays, reading instructions from cards, reading their own writing, reading letters and helping friends to read together. The 'read to the teacher time', however, is special because it generally lasts a fairly long time and its main purpose is to attend to the reader's strengths and weaknesses. Therefore, if this time is to be successful, it needs careful planning on the part of the teacher.

Where should the teacher start?

It is essential to build upon a child's existing knowledge of literacy and not to presume that all children of the same age will have reached a similar stage of understanding.

An interview with the parent before the child starts school should provide good background knowledge and answer questions such as the following:

- Has the child had lots of stories read to her?
- Does the child like to look at books?
- Does the child have a favourite book?
- Does the child pretend to read a favourite book, turning the pages at the appropriate time?
- Is the child already reading?
- Does the child have any books of her own?

This liaison with parents is covered further in Chapter 14, 'Using parents wisely'.

When first sharing a book with the reception child, it is essential that both the child and the teacher feel safe and comfortable. As far as possible, this time should be free from interruptions from other children. If others need attention, encourage them to sit nearby and share the book

as well, and help them to appreciate that this is *not* a time to interrupt. It is not uncommon to find a circle of interested onlookers sharing the story by the time a teacher has finished!

During this time much can be learned from gentle observation.

• Does the child handle the book with confidence?

• Does the child know where to turn to in order to start the reading?

• Does the child know how to turn the pages?

• Does the child stop and offer comments about the pictures or the story or both?

• Do you feel that the child is happy with a book?

Where should the teacher and child sit?

Most classrooms now have a 'book corner' that has a comfortable seat of some kind in it, and this would seem a natural place to use. However, if the teacher is the only adult in the room this might prove impractical if she is unable to see the rest of the class. Many teachers prefer the child to come up to her desk and stand beside her to read. While this may be necessary from the point of view of classroom control, it might seem very daunting to a new child. A solution could be to have two chairs side by side *near* this focal point and for the teacher to establish that when she is sitting on the 'reading' chair she does not want to be interrupted.

Tavener (1985) suggests that the child and the teacher should work at the same level, as this ensures a clear vision of the book for both participants and also creates a feeling of unity. Remember that it is essential that the child sees himself as in control of the book. The child should hold the book, turn the pages and finally put the book back on a shelf or into the 'going home bag'. Far too often the teacher dominates the session and the child becomes a passive observer.

Hearing the 'emergent' reader

It has been clearly established that children need to see reading as meaningful, pleasurable and worthwhile. Many children need to hear and experience stories for some considerable time before they are ready to tackle print. This experience can be offered through sharing a 'big book' with a group and during story time with the class. However, sharing a story, poem or picture book is equally essential in individual reading time, for the child who is not familiar with stories. The child needs to realise that books make sense and to talk with the teacher about the story, perhaps discovering that they have both experienced losing something, have a naughty pet or have been to the seaside. The child needs to bring knowledge *to* a text and to receive satisfaction *from* a text in order to become a reader. He can begin to retell a story, join in with repeated phrases and link the spoken word to the marks on the page.

As the child grows in understanding about books and the way they work, he moves towards the time when he needs to begin to tackle the print. The teacher needs to ensure that the child fully understands what he is doing while he reads. Showing the child where to start to read, running a finger under the words as they are read, stopping to discuss the pictures or the story and talking about such things as punctuation and the spaces between words, all help him to begin to understand the many functions of print.

Hearing the beginning reader

' "Can you read, Pooh?" he asked a little anxiously. "There's a notice about knocking and ringing outside my door, which Christopher Robin wrote. Could you read it?"

"Christopher Robin told me what it said, then I could." ' A.A. Milne, *The House at Pooh Corner* (Methuen).

As children take over responsibility for tackling the text, it is quite usual for them to concentrate so hard on the words that they fail to follow the story. This does not mean that they are incapable of understanding the text, but rather that their efforts have concentrated on the words at the expense of comprehension. Reading the text to the child and discussing the story before expecting the child to read it ensures that she brings meaning to the text and allows her to offer sensible guesses for an unknown word.

At this very early stage, many teachers find reading in unison with the child creates a feeling of success and relieves much of the tension that can build up so easily with the beginning reader. This approach has been called a 'paired reading' method, and is one that many parents find much more acceptable than the more passive traditional approach of hearing their child read and only intervening when he stumbles over a word. As the child comes to read more and more text, the teacher can begin to hold back from providing every 'difficult' word, encouraging the child to tackle the text. If, however, the teacher always provides the answer, the child will come to rely on help every time. This has sometimes been referred to as 'look and say': the child *looks* at the adult and the adult *says* the word!

At this stage, the teacher should begin to suggest strategies that will help the reader to access the text when reading without the ready support of an adult. For example, many children approach an unknown word very slowly, almost hoping it

The Birthday Party

will go away. In such a case, it often helps to persuade the reader to read up to the word again at speed. We are more likely to predict a word if we approach it reading with expression and pace. If this approach does not help the child to produce the word, the teacher can persuade her to read beyond the word. Often the rest of the sentence or passage will make the meaning of the word clear, and this may in turn produce recognition of the word. Very often the reader suddenly exclaims, 'Oh, that must say "surprise" ' and then instinctively goes back to the beginning of the sentence and rereads it. If this strategy fails, the child could be persuaded to examine the illustrations for clues. It is frequently the nouns that are unfamiliar, and these are often illustrated. If this still fails and the reader is losing confidence, she should be persuaded to return to the beginning of the sentence and then use letter/sound attack. As adults, we hope that by pronouncing a word we may recognise it. Young readers can also be encouraged to try to decode the word, and if the word is then recognised, the

reading may continue. However, by this time the child may have lost the sense of the text, and the teacher may need to read up to the word and encourage the child to try to read it in context and then carry on. Obviously, if telling the child does not lead to understanding, then the teacher must be 'the dictionary' and talk about the meaning of the word.

Sometimes, the teacher may decide to try to draw the child's attention to 'problem' words at the end of the reading time. However, it is very difficult to read a word out of context, so stabbing a finger at a word with which a child has already had difficulty is hardly likely to lead to a successful attempt. On the other hand, asking the child to find the word on the page can be much more positive. In this situation the child generally rereads the text and then finds the word

through a combination of memory recall and the sense of the passage. This both encourages the child to pay attention to the word and goes some way towards consolidating the vocabulary.

Keeping a brief record of the ways in which the child approaches unknown vocabulary will help the teacher to provide games and activities to consolidate these words. (See Chapter 4, pages 41 to 45, and Chapter 5, pages 53 to 56.)

It cannot be stressed too much that if the teacher gives the impression that all she wants is a 'perfect' reading of the words, then many children

In the illustration: Our Farm Visit — the farmer was nice — Chi — Sammy — I like the sheep best — I saw some pigs — dean

will provide this and only this. Being able to discuss what you have read is just as important as reading the words. Indeed, as children become more and more fluent, discussing and commenting on the text becomes more important. If neither the child nor the teacher can find anything that requires comment, then it may be time to look more carefully at the book and to consider whether it is worth keeping.

Running records

As the child moves towards fluency, the teacher needs to use some of the time while hearing the child read to make 'running records'. These are so called because the teacher marks the text while the child is reading. The teacher has either a replica of the text the child is reading or a perspex sheet placed over a second copy of the book. The idea is to tick every word that is read correctly, and when errors occur, to mark what the reader says or does.

The child might at first find this offputting, so discussion and explanation of what the teacher is doing is essential. Children usually get used to this procedure quickly, but if marking during the reading seems to disturb the child's understanding, then taping the reading session can be used as an alternative.

The advantages of keeping running records are as follows:

• They give the teacher an accurate record of the reader's approaches to the text.
• They show clearly what a child can do as opposed to what he cannot do. There are always more ticks above a text than comment letters.
• Records deal with a text the child is reading in the normal course of events, and thus the assessment is not presented in a 'test' form.
• They provide specific information about the strategies a child is using. Published tests frequently test only one aspect of the reading process, and this may not be the strategy the child is using.
• Records quickly show the teacher when a child is beginning to struggle so that she can intervene before despair and disillusionment set in.

Marking the running record

The procedure for marking a running record is as follows.
• Tick every word correctly identified.

- Self-correction: write the word first offered by the child above the text word. If the child self-corrects, write the letters SC beside them.
- Initial sound: if the child sounds the word in any way, write these sounds above the word.
- Omissions: place an O over any words that are omitted. If the omission seems to affect the meaning of the text, provide the missing word and mark the text as for 'intervention'.
- Intervention: sometimes it is necessary to intervene, especially if the meaning of the passage is lost. Reread the misread text and if the child is able to continue with understanding, allow her to do so. Mark this text with a line above it and the letter I.

An example of a running record is given in Figure 1.

This example illustrates twelve hesitations or deviations from the text. The child is reading with 90 per cent accuracy and therefore the text can be considered suitable for the child to share with the teacher. An analysis of the miscues would be as follows:

returned/came. The child is reading for meaning, but does not notice deviation.

wondering/w...w...when. The child is self-correcting, but repeating the same error. He then tries sound attack, but loses the meaning and the teacher intervenes.

home/house. The child substitutes 'house', but the teacher ignores this as the meaning is not impaired.

gloomy. Intervention by the teacher is needed as the child makes no attempt at the word.

pushed/omitted. The word is not essential to text; its omission could be an oversight. The teacher could draw attention to this after the read has finished.

open/opened. The child involuntarily offers the correct syntax.

their/the. The child self-corrects.

home/house. The child self-corrects.

demanded/asked. The child offers a good alternative word and again does not seem to

---

When the dwarfs returned [came] home they saw that the door of their cottage was open. They crept up to the door, wondering [w...w...when] who could have found their home [house]. They looked in through the window but it was gloomy [I] inside and they could not see Snow White. At last they pushed open [O opened] the door. Someone had been eating their [s.c. the] food and someone had been drinking their milk.

"Who can have found our home [s.c. house]?" demanded [asked] the tallest dwarf.

Just then the youngest [y...y...] dwarf called out, "Someone is asleep on my bed. She is the prettiest [s.c. best] person I have ever seen. Come quickly [O] and see."

All the dwarfs ran up the stairs and at that moment Snow White woke up.

Figure 1

notice the deviation.

youngest/y...y... Teacher intervention is necessary as the child loses meaning after a long hesitation.

prettiest/best. The child self-corrects.

quickly/omitted. This omission results in little loss of meaning.

In conclusion, this passage is at the correct level for the reader to read aloud. He is reading for meaning but could now afford to pay more attention to the actual text. The reader needs to be encouraged to read on when meeting an unknown word rather than stopping too long and losing the meaning.

Analysing running records

It is easiest to calculate an error rate using marks out of twenty. That is, if a child only stumbles on one word in every twenty, she is reading with 95 per cent accuracy. When reading alone, a minimum of 95 per cent is necessary. If the child constantly offers this amount of accuracy in the one-to-one reading session, then it is unlikely that the material will enable the teacher to offer any constructive help. When reading to the teacher, 90 to 95 per cent accuracy is considered to be at the correct instructional level. Below 90 per cent the child easily becomes frustrated and may begin to make so many errors that it is impossible to decide which are the result of the difficulty of the text and which are poor reading strategies. If the child achieves below 90 per cent accuracy, the text is not at the right level for the reader.

Interpreting 'self-correction'

Mistakes with no self-correction

If the reader deviates from the text and reads words that do not make sense (or words that do not exist) and does not appear to realise what he is doing, then intervention is essential. The child has either not understood that reading should be meaningful or is concentrating so hard on the production of words that he is not processing the text for its meaning. In such a case, the teacher should take over the

text and either read it to the child or suggest that they read it together.

Poor self-correction

Some children realise they have misread the text and self-correct, but they do so inaccurately, often offering the same error. These children do not seem to seek meaning in their self-correction. Although this is not as serious as the child who does not appear to notice the error, it is still a serious situation and the teacher needs to intervene and draw attention to the correct reading of the text.

Alternative self-correction

Sometimes a child realises that she has misread, and self-corrects with an alternative word that manages to keep the meaning of the passage intact. If the teacher intervenes and points out that she has made an error, the child may quickly become a 'word' reader, seeking for accuracy rather than reading for meaning. Write the word the child offers above the text and discuss the choice and accuracy after the child has finished reading. It may have been a slip of the tongue, the word may have been outside the child's vocabulary, or the text may have broken the child's subconscious rules so that she has instinctively corrected it. This can happen when children are reading text written in dialect which may have deliberately broken orthodox grammar. For example, ' "I goes down the road to me friend" said the old man' might be changed by a young reader to 'I went down the road to my friend'. The child is obviously reading for meaning but is not paying careful attention to the text. The teacher could discuss this after the child has finished reading.

Accurate self-correction

Children who self-correct accurately are reading for meaning and hearing themselves read. This strategy needs both praise and encouragement. Teachers have to be careful that they do not intervene too quickly with these readers. It is all too easy to provide the word because the child has misread and to leave insufficient time for self-correction. It has been suggested by Glynn (1980) that twelve seconds can be allowed to elapse before the teacher needs to intervene. This can seem like a life-time in the busy classroom, but certainly at least five seconds is not unreasonable.

Using a tape recorder

If a child is uneasy with the teacher marking a running record on paper, using a tape recorder might prove a good alternative.

Choose a place near an electric plug and if possible use an electric lead for the power source, as batteries can be very expensive. Put a chair against the wall and a table or desk in front of it on which to place the tape recorder. This will ensure that no child can walk behind the reader while taping is being undertaken.

Ensure that the child is settled and happy with the choice of reading material and ready to start reading. Label the tape with the child's name, the date and the title of the book. Ten-minute tapes are ideal for this purpose, and avoid time being spent searching for the end of the previous recording, as tends to happen when using a 60-minute tape.

The recording should be done in the classroom, but it is important to ensure that the voice of the reader is the major input and that the usual classroom buzz does not interfere with the recording.

Encouraging reflection

It is vital that children are taught to reflect on the meaning of what they have read if they are to become competent and confident readers. The following procedure could be used when reading with a child to encourage reflection:
• Give the child the opportunity to look over what has been read.
• Ask the child to show you the funniest/most interesting/most frightening picture.
• Prompt recall by asking questions such as, 'Did you like the bit when...?
• Ask the child what she would have done in a similar situation.

CHAPTER 8

Links between reading & writing

'As children read more, write more, discuss what they have read and move through the range of writing in English, they amass a store of images from half remembered poems, of lines from plays, of phrases, rhythms and ideas. Such a reception of language allows the individual greater possibilities of production of language.' (DES, 1988)

The links between reading and writing are very strong, since what a reader reads influences what she writes. Successful writing cannot be achieved unless the writer has heard, read and talked about texts that provide good models both of fiction and of non-fiction.

BACKGROUND

We are all aware of the way phrases of poems or stories, snatches of songs, advertising jingles and quotations slip almost unbidden into our minds. How did they get there? What do we do with them? These snippets and strings of words have become part of our language repertoire because, from our earliest years, we have been surrounded by such things.

Today many children learn a great deal about language patterns and rhythms from the television. In fact, television jingles and slogans could probably be considered as modern nursery rhymes. Like the traditional nursery rhymes before them, they describe important aspects of our culture.

As we become familiar with the language all around us, so we begin to use it in speech, and then gradually in writing and reading. Through a great deal of practice and experimentation, young

children gradually become fluent speakers. As they begin to talk, they learn about language and how to make their meaning clear. Similarly, children draw on their knowledge about language as they begin to write.

The combination of practice and experience helps children understand how to create meaning both in speech and in writing. When learning to read, knowledge about language helps children to understand the meaning of the text. As young children hear stories and look at and share books, so they begin to acquire 'writerly knowledge'. Without these experiences, the complex act of composing and writing is difficult. Coupled with these experiences, children need to be helped to understand that writing is done for a purpose and that it has value for a reader.

Starting school

Children come to school with many different experiences of reading and writing. Some children will have had stories read to them or will have seen stories told on television. They may even be able to read some of these texts. They may also have had many opportunities to write in various contexts, such as helping with the shopping list, sending a greetings card or writing a letter. Other children may start school without having had these experiences. However, they may have had equally valid potential literary experiences, such as being told about the childhood of their parents, about how cars work, about things they see on the way to the shops and by being involved in family discussions. It is through such dialogues that the child makes sense of the world and comes to an understanding of story.

It is important to remember this range of experiences when introducing children to the tools and methods of literacy at school. If the children's home culture is not reflected in the culture of the school, then children may well have difficulties in recognising the important and central role that reading and writing play in school.

The teacher's role

It is essential to establish the literacy experiences that the child is bringing to school, and it is important not to make assumptions. Observe the child in various classroom contexts, and encourage him to talk about things that interest him or things about which he is curious. Frequently children new to school will be puzzled by language and actions that we take for granted, such as 'face the front', 'put it in the cloakroom' or 'go and line up'.

Note down any observation that is particularly pertinent.

Remember that the information that parents have given in the pre-school interview can provide insights into children's literacy experiences and enable teachers to avoid undermining the children's existing knowledge. For example, a child who has been described as 'enjoying helping' should be given a similar opportunity in school before being shown how his activities could be written down and read about.

Provide as many opportunities as possible for children to behave like readers and writers. Encourage them to 'write' shopping lists when playing shops, to 'read' to the teddy in the book corner, and to tell stories to each other and to the class.

Similarities between reading and writing

The language links between reading and writing can be considered in terms of what readers and writers do while engaged in those two activities. A child will bring to his reading a knowledge of:

• the topic;
• the language appropriate to the topic (for example fiction/non-fiction);
• sound/symbol relationships;
• previous reading experiences;
• text organisation;
• the purposes for reading and the needs of a reader.

Similarly, a writer brings to her writing a knowledge of:
• the topic;
• the language appropriate to the topic (for example fiction/non-fiction);
• sound/symbol relationships;
• previous reading and writing experiences;
• the audience and purposes for their writing.

During reading, readerly behaviour involves:
• draft reading (skimming, scanning, predicting);
• rereading (to revise opinion, clarify understanding);

• taking account of writing conventions to aid understanding (such as titles, sub-headings, punctuation, spelling).

During writing, writerly behaviour involves:
• draft writing (notes, plans, diagrams);
• redrafting or rewriting (eg to revise, clarify meaning);
• taking account of readers' needs (such as titles, sub-headings, punctuation, spelling).

After reading, a reader:
• reflects on what has been read;
• often wants to talk about and discuss what he has been reading;
• feels satisfaction.

After writing, a writer:
• reflects on what has been written;
• may discuss her writing with a 'response partner' (a partner who has read the writing and who discusses it with the writer);
• feels satisfaction.

ACTIVITIES

1. Questions to the class

Age range
Five to seven.

Group size
The whole class.

What you need
A flipchart or board, a variety of writing implements.

What to do
Put the flipchart or board where it is easily accessible and leave a variety of writing implements nearby.

In the centre or along the top of the sheet, write a question appropriate to a book the children have read, such as 'What do you think the giant would like for his dinner?' or 'What things have you noticed about any bird you have seen?'

Explain to the children that this question needs answering and that you will leave the paper up for two or three days. Invite the children to write or draw their suggestions and observations.

At an appropriate time, discuss with the class all the contributions, encouraging them to justify their remarks.

2. Write your own version

Age range
Five to seven.

Group size
The whole class.

What you need
A favourite story, a large sheet of paper or board, suitable writing implements, a computer.

What to do
Choose a favourite classroom story and read or tell it to the children. Stories that have a clear and strong framework work best, such as *The Very Hungry Caterpillar*, Eric Carle (Picture Puffin), *Don't Forget the Bacon*, Pat Hutchins (Picture Puffin) or 'Goldilocks' (traditional tale). Discuss the characters and story events.

Suggest to the group that they make a new version, using the basic structure of the story. Invite suggestions as to how the children could make their own story, based on the one they have just heard. Write down these suggestions on a large sheet of paper or on the board so that all the children can see what you are doing. As the children work on their story, retell the original from time to time so that they can hear if their story is following the pattern of the model.

Let the children decide how to 'publish' this story. For example, they could choose to make one large book with the text written by an adult and illustrations by members of the

class, or they might want to type the story on to the computer so that each child has his own copy to illustrate.

3. Notice this

Age range
Five to seven.

Group size
Pairs.

What you need
Large sheets of paper, a range of writing and drawing implements, scissors.

What to do
Talk to the children about the different notices that they can see around the school and in the environment.

Ask the children to work in pairs to design a notice that they think would be useful in the classroom. Provide them with large sheets of paper and a range of writing and drawing implements. Let the children display their notices in the appropriate places in the classroom.

4. An instant big book

Age range
Five to seven.

Group size
The whole class, working in pairs.

What you need
An old wall display, sheets of A3 paper, adhesive, staples, thread or slide binders, card, felt-tipped pens.

What to do
On most infant classroom walls there are thematic displays of children's drawing and writing. These can easily be converted into a 'big book'. Discuss the display with the children and encourage them to decide how it could be organised to make a book.

Divide the display material into the appropriate number of pages, and provide pairs of children with a sheet of A3 paper for each page. Ask the pairs to decide how to arrange their material on the page.

Discuss with each pair how they have organised their layout before allowing them to stick the display material on to the large sheets of paper. When each page is complete, let the whole class discuss the order in which they should be assembled. When this has been established, let the children put the pages in the correct order.

Let the children decide on a title for the book. Choose substantial card to make the cover and write the agreed title on to this card. (The children may like to add illustrations to the cover.) Where possible,

follow publishing conventions by adding the names of the authors or the editors and the date of publication.

Finally staple or bind the cover and the pages together and share this book with the class.

5. Read the picture, read the word

Age range
Five to seven.

Group size
The whole class, working individually.

What you need
A well-known story, paper, pens, coloured pencils or crayons, scissors, adhesive.

What to do
Retell a well-known tale, such as Red Riding Hood, to the class. Talk about how this could be written as a picture story so that all the class could read it. For example, the following words could all be illustrated: Red Riding Hood; Mother; Path; Flowers; Basket; Wolf; Grandma; Woodcutter.

Write the story in clear print on a large piece of paper, so that all the children can see it. Read the words as you write them so that the children can clearly see the correspondence between the print and the spoken word.

When the story is complete, highlight all those words that could be represented by a picture.

Give each child a piece of paper that will easily cover a highlighted word, then ask them to choose a word to illustrate.

When the illustrations are complete, stick them in place over the words, applying adhesive only to the top edge of the illustration so that the picture flaps can be lifted to disclose the word when needed. Let the children share this 'book'.

6. Book making

Age range
Five to seven.

Group size
Individuals or pairs.

What you need
Paper, writing implements.

What to do
The advantage of this method of making books is that it is very simple and, as it requires

Figure 1

> 1. Fold one coloured A4 sheet in half to make the cover.
>
>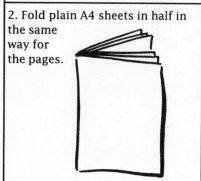
>
> 2. Fold plain A4 sheets in half in the same way for the pages.
>
>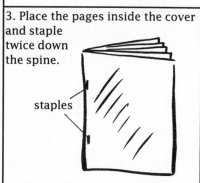
>
> 3. Place the pages inside the cover and staple twice down the spine.
>
> staples

Figure 2

> 1. Proceed as for Figure 1, but cut the paper to make a triangle shape.
>
>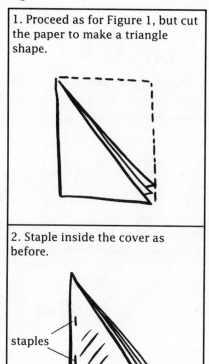
>
> 2. Staple inside the cover as before.
>
> staples

Figure 3

> For a lift-the-flap book, proceed as for Figure 1, but use two sheets of A4 for each of the pages. Cut flaps in the top sheet and stick it on to the underneath sheet so the flaps can be opened to reveal words or pictures underneath.
>
>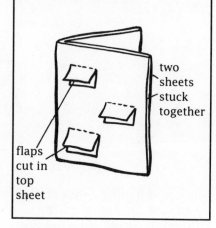
>
> two sheets stuck together
>
> flaps cut in top sheet

very little cutting, it can be done by the youngest children. Being so straightforward it allows children to produce books for their own writing on a regular basis.

Show or help the children to fold their paper as in Figures 1 to 3. Ask them to work either individually or in pairs. Let them use the paper to write something of their own choice, such as a story, information, jokes or riddles.

Ask the children to put the author's and illustrator's names on the cover.

7. Story building

Age range
Five to seven.

Group size
The whole class.

What you need
A large sheet of paper or a board, appropriate writing implements.

What to do
This game builds on children's knowledge of stories. Divide the paper or board into four columns. The first, third and fourth columns need to be quite wide. The second column (which will always have the word 'met' in it) can be narrow.

Provide a story framework

by writing above the columns 'Who', 'Met', 'Who' and 'Where'.

Encourage the children to talk about any fairy stories that they know. Discuss the characters' names with the group.

Ask the children which character they would like to choose to put in the first column, then write the name for the children to see. Discuss with them who their chosen character might meet and where the meeting might take place. Write their suggestions in the appropriate columns.

Read the resulting 'mini-stories' to the group. These stories can be used as a basis for talking about characters and plot development. Possible stories might include:
• Little Red Riding Hood met the Three Little Pigs in a wood;
• Cinderella met Foxy Loxy in Grandma's cottage;
• The Hungry Caterpillar met Tom and Lucy in a dark, dark wood.

CHAPTER 9

Reading aloud to the class

Reading aloud to young children is a daily activity in most schools. Very few children in the reception and Y1 and Y2 classes are able to read well enough by themselves, and a tradition has grown up that these children should be read to every day. Many teachers look forward to this time as the children enjoy it so much. Furthermore, it is a way of settling a class down before they go home! However, it is only recently that the real value of reading to children has been recognised and its importance as a regular part of the school day seen as so much more than 'a lovely time'.

Reading stories

Why should children hear stories every day?

Reading aloud is the best way to share a book with a class or an individual child. Much of a child's experience of books in the classroom comprises the private sharing between child and adult. In contrast to this, reading to a group of children provides them with a common experience and this can form a mutual bond between the listeners. They can talk about the book and, in reliving the humorous parts and anticipating what might happen next, they can retell and re-enact the story. In this way they receive a glimpse of the real reason for reading and come to understand that books are there waiting to be enjoyed, offering the opportunity of entering another world. Through adult mediation the children are able to share in a world of stories which goes far beyond their reading ability.

By reading to the children, the teacher demonstrates her own love of books and transmits her enthusiasm to the class. When the teacher reads with pace, intonation and expression, the children both hear and see how a confident adult reads a book. Thus they are presented with a model which they will later be able to emulate. Frequently a child will ask to read the book the teacher has just read to the class, and will imitate her teacher's voice at the appropriate points.

When the teacher reads aloud to the class, she gives the children the opportunity to experience stories which are at the right level emotionally, but which might be far too difficult for them to read alone. The class may laugh together at some of the antics of the characters, and through the shared laughter, come to experience some of the power of books. In a similar way, children can experience sorrow, joy, excitement and even a slight frisson of fear. By reading aloud to the class, the teacher is able to control and orchestrate the emotions evoked by the book. Often teachers will use a book to enable children to understand the problems of others.

In reading the book to the class, the teacher is also able to demonstrate the way a book works. When hearing a child read, there is rarely enough time to check continually that

he has understood all the literary conventions, but by constantly drawing attention to these when reading aloud, the teacher can help children to become familiar with them.

Children can be prepared for selecting books for themselves with more confidence in the future by:
• talking about the title and the clue it gives to the contents of the book;
• discussing the author and reminding the children of other books by the same person;
• encouraging them to look at the illustrations and showing how the illustrator has added little bits of information that were not in the text.

Similarly, the teacher demonstrates the conventions of print, by showing the class where she is reading, how to hold a book and how to turn the pages. Above all, by reading to the children the teacher begins to give the listeners a sense of story, familiarising them with story form. Later they may even write a story which follows the same structure as a story they have heard.

What makes a book suitable for reading aloud?

Although a teacher can never be certain of the exact amount of time she might have for reading aloud, having a rough idea will affect the choice of reading matter.

Often, with reception children, a quick read of a complete story is the best use of the time. The story should not be too complex. Children who have not had stories read to them before they come to school cannot cope with too many characters or too devious a plot. They need to hear about familiar events in stories to provide a common experience which can allow them to begin to relate to the story.

Children frequently love to hear the same story several times, and traditional stories are generally firm favourites. If a retelling allows the group to join in the story, perhaps by chanting a familiar refrain, such as 'Who's been sitting on my chair?' or 'I'll huff and I'll puff and I'll blow your house down', then the children come to feel that they are part of the story and begin to make it their own. If possible, such a reading session should be offered at least once a week to new reception children.

Nowadays, illustrations are often such an important part of the book that it is difficult to understand what is happening without referring to them. When reading to the whole class it may not be possible for all the children to see these clues, so care needs to be taken with texts in which the meaning depends upon the pictures. For this reason it is always best to read the book first before offering it to a class. Perhaps the books that

work best are those which can be read aloud without needing constant reference to the pictures. This enables the listeners to attend carefully to the story and imagine for themselves. If undue attention is given to the pictures many children forget to listen to the story and look only at the picture. Then they will all too often quickly become inattentive and restless. A way round this is to read the page or the whole story without showing the illustration and then to let the children see what the artist imagined. This can lead to many comments and exclamations of surprise.

When should a teacher read aloud?

Traditionally the most popular time for reading aloud is the end of the afternoon. Reading to the children at the end of the day is rather like reading to a child before bedtime – it provides a time of quiet and calm. As the true value of reading aloud has become recognised, it is now seen as something which should be offered at many different times of the day. This approach has the obvious advantage of allowing a teacher to read part of a story and to have time to discuss it before completing it later in the day.

What texts should a teacher use?

It is always best to try to offer as wide a variety of texts as possible. These could include:
• rhyming texts that encourage children to participate;
• stories with lots of repetition;
• stories that mirror the kind of activities the children experience in everyday life;
• stories about favourite characters;
• traditional stories;
• sad stories;
• humorous stories;
• stories the children have written;
• stories the teacher has written;
• short and long poems;
• simple information texts;
• historical stories;
• stories about the environment;
• nursery rhymes.

Read alouds for reception children

Stories and information

Berg, Leila (1986) *Time for One More*, Methuen/Magnet.
Blake, Quentin (1980) *Mr Magnolia*, Cape/Armada Picture Lions.
Burningham, John (1970) *Mr Gumpy's Outing*, Cape/Picture Puffin.

Corrin, Sara and Corrin, Stephen (Ed.) (1973) *Stories for Five Year Olds and Other Young Readers*, Faber/Puffin.
Dodd, Lynley, the Hairy Maclary stories, Spindlewood/ Picture Puffin.
Edwards, Dorothy (1969) *My Naughty Little Sister*, Methuen/ Magnet.
Faulkner, Keith and Adams, Georgie (1985) *The Cat Sat on the Rat*, Beehive/Macdonald.
Hughes, Shirley (1988) *The Big Alfie and Annie Rose Story Book*, Bodley Head.
Miller, Jane (1986) *Seasons on the Farm*, Dent.
Murphy, Jill (1980) *Peace at Last*, Picturemac.
Russell, Naomi (1989) *The Oak – The Mysterious Life of a Tree*, Methuen.
Winthrop, Elizabeth (1987) *Shoes*, Gollancz.

Poetry

Blake, Quentin (1991) *All Join In*, Cape.
Cherry, Lynne (1988) *Who's Sick Today?*, Andersen Press.
Foster, John (1988) *Another First Poetry Book*, Oxford University Press.
Royds, Caroline (Ed.) (1986) *Read Me a Poem*, Kingfisher.

Read alouds for Y1 and Y2

Stories and information

Briggs, Raymond (1974) *The Fairy Tale Treasury*, Puffin.
Corrin, Sara and Corrin, Stephen (1967) *Stories for Six Year Olds and Other Young Readers*, Faber/Puffin.
Flournoy, Valerie (1985) *The Patchwork Quilt*, Bodley Head/ Picture Puffin.
Grant, John (1985) BBC/Knight, *Little Nose and Two Eyes*, Hodder & Stoughton.
Heaslip, Peter (1987) *Grandma's Favourite*, Methuen.

Impey, Rose (1989) *A letter to Father Christmas*, Orchard Books.
Jackman, Wayne (1990) *Woolly Hat*, Wayland.
Jennings, Terry (1988) *Earthworms*, Oxford University Press.
Jessel, Camilla (1990) *If You Meet a Stranger*, Walker.
Joy, Margaret (1987) *Allotment Lane School Again*, Puffin.
Jungman, Ann (1989) *The Little Dragon Steps Out*, Corgi.
Keller, Holly (1987) *Lizzie's Invitation*, Julia MacRae Books/ Walker.
Murphy, Jill (1978) *The Worst Witch*, Puffin.
Oldfield, Pamela (1977) *The Terribly Plain Princess*, Hodder & Stoughton/Beaver.
Richardson, Jean and Carey, Joanna (1988) *A Dog For Ben*, Methuen/Puffin.
Ross, Tony (1987) *Stone Soup*, Anderson Press/Beaver.
Smith, Dick (1989) *Sophie's Snail*, Walker Books.
Viorst, Judith *The Tenth Good Thing About Barney*, Collins.

Poetry

Agard, John (1984) *I Din Do Nuttin*, Bodley Head/Magnet.
Bennet, Jill (1989) *A Pot of Gold*, Doubleday.
Royds, Caroline (Ed.) (1986) *Read Me a Poem*, Kingfisher.

ACTIVITIES

1. Saying the rhyme

Age range
Five to eight.

Group size
The whole class.

What you need
Books of poetry, nursery rhymes or any book that has a rhyming refrain, such as *Hairy Maclary from Donaldson's Dairy* by Lynley Dodd (Spindlewood/Puffin 1985).

What to do
Read through the text together and encourage the children to join in as they pick up the notion of the repeated refrain.

At the end of the first reading suggest that all the group join in with the refrain, and then reread the text.

At the end of this reading divide the group into smaller units and give each of these either a part of the refrain or a complete line to say aloud, for example, 'and Bottomly Potts all covered in spots' or 'and Hairy Maclary from Donaldson's Dairy'.

Extend this for as long as the group are able to remember the different lines. It is an excellent way of introducing 'learning by heart', which young children seem to find so easy and so satisfying.

2. Who am I?

Age range
Five to eight.

Group size
The whole class.

What you need
A retelling of a traditional story with a range of characters, such as the Three Billy Goats Gruff, Goldilocks and the Three Bears, the Three Little Pigs, Jack and the Beanstalk.

What to do
Read the story aloud to the group and emphasise the different voices that can be used for each character.

Reread the story, but this time select different children to represent the different characters. When the characters occur in the text, encourage the appropriate child to stand up and say either 'that's me' or, if they are able, say the full sentence (for example, 'Who's been sitting

Who's been sitting in my chair?

on my chair?' or 'Fee, fi, fo, fum'). Encourage them to try to speak in the character's voice.

Finally, let the group enact the story for other classes, visitors or parents.

3. Noises off

Age range
Five to eight.

Group size
The whole class.

What you need
A story that calls for a range of sound effects.

What to do
Read the story through to the group. Ask the children how they could make the 'noises off' for the story. Encourage responses such as the following:
• stamping with their feet for walking;
• blowing into their hands to represent wind;
• rubbing their hands together to represent water;
• clapping for various situations such as horses galloping;
• rubbing their hands on their clothes for walking through grass;
• snoring to represent sleep;
• drumming with their fingers to represent rain.

Reread the story again, letting the group make the appropriate noises. This is very popular and often requires several rereadings.

Some good titles for this are:
Mr Gumpy's Motor Car, John Burningham (Picture Puffin).
Rosie's Walk, Pat Hutchins (Picture Puffin).
The Gingerbread Boy, Traditional (Usborne).
Burglar Bill, Allan Ahlberg, (Armada Picture Lions).
Mr Magnolia, Quentin Blake (Picture Lions).
Meg and Mog, Helen Nicoll and Jan Pienkowski (Heinemann).

CHAPTER 10

Becoming an independent reader

The purpose of teaching children to read is to enable them to turn to books for information and enjoyment throughout their lives. Many children make an excellent start at the early stages of reading but then seem to reach a plateau in their reading ability beyond which they find it very difficult to progress. They may have shown signs of appreciating the importance of the various cueing strategies necessary in reading; they may have enjoyed making progress through the structured programme offered in reception and Y1 and then, just when we hope they will develop into fully fledged readers, they seem to struggle with texts, lose confidence, lose enthusiasm and eventually become disappointingly poor readers. Why does this occur?

BACKGROUND

It is possible that what has happened is that the child has become over-dependent upon the teacher to provide rewards (in the form of praise) for success. What frequently happens is that the teacher spends less time hearing the reading of a child who is making good progress, reserving that time for those children whose progress is not so swift. For some children, this 'casting off' into free reading is not welcomed as much by them as it is by the teacher.

How can we avoid this syndrome?

First of all, we can ensure that the child's first experiences of reading alone do not occur only in Y2. Children who have been encouraged to develop as readers by being allowed to discover the pleasures of browsing through books and by enjoying a solo read are far less likely to feel abandoned.

Secondly, we can maintain a high interest in children as readers. This may not take the form of hearing them read, but instead we will spend time with them discussing books, suggesting books to choose and providing the opportunity for stories to be read together in small groups, thus enabling children to share the pleasures of their developing skill in reading.

In this way, children can gradually relinquish their dependence upon the teacher always hearing them read, as they will have experienced some sense of independence in reading long before they are fully independent readers.

Characteristics of the independent reader

Choosing books

One of the skills of successful reading is being able to select books efficiently for one's individual needs. This is not a skill children automatically acquire as their reading ability improves; it is something they need to experience alongside their developing ability. Children need to be shown how to make decisions about books (see Activity 3, page 104). Obviously, too much choice can baffle the newly fluent reader, but as children become more discriminating we can widen the choice on offer.

Silent reading

This characteristic of reading is one that some children adopt effortlessly, while others relinquish reading aloud very reluctantly. One seven-year-old

girl said to her teacher, 'How do I know what I've read if I haven't said it?'

It is possible that too much reading aloud to the teacher might inhibit the development of the skill of reading silently. Children need time to discover the pleasures of silent reading. The opportunity to spend time quietly reading needs to be part of the daily experience of the newly fluent reader.

Reading widely

The child who feels confident of his success in reading will choose to read material of varying levels of difficulty. He will feel sufficiently confident to tackle material that is a challenge to read. Equally, independent readers are not so reliant upon the level of the book to denote their status as readers. Less confident readers are sometimes reluctant to read an 'easy' book as they depend heavily upon the level of the book to communicate to themselves and others precisely where they stand as readers. They are afraid of being associated with a low level of reading ability and assume that good readers only read 'difficult' books. In order to encourage independence in

reading, teachers need to provide a role model of enjoyment of reading at various levels of difficulty.

Independent readers also move freely between reading fiction for pleasure and reading non-fiction for information. Although the skills of non-fiction reading are essentially developed in children aged eight and over, the preparation for this begins much earlier. Children who have experienced a wide range of reading material will have expectations about different texts and will be beginning to appreciate the different styles involved when switching from fiction to non-fiction. In order to prepare children for this, teachers should regularly read non-fiction to them, thereby showing them the importance of reading the text reflectively if they are to hold on to the information.

Interpretation while reading

Independent readers move easily from book experience to

life experience and vice versa. They will constantly make comparisons or contrasts between the world of the book and their own lives, and will be able to interpret experience with the benefit of both worlds. In this respect, independent readers are in control of their reading. They give and receive ideas freely. Less fluent readers, however, are servants of the text. They are satisfied if they have accurately read the words.

In order to foster an exchange of ideas between reader and text, teachers need to provide plenty of opportunities to share books in groups or with partners. In this way we emphasise the importance of taking meaning beyond the printed word. Once children have experienced the pleasure of extracting meaning and information from texts for the benefit of others, they will

> Maria came in through the wall. She could hear the sound of crying....

appreciate the importance of doing so for themselves when reading privately.

Understanding punctuation

Many young readers fail to comprehend texts, not because of difficult vocabulary, but because their syntactic knowledge is poor and so they ignore punctuation. If punctuation is ignored it is often almost impossible to make sense of what is written. Consider the difference between the following sentences:

• 'Mary,' said Jane, 'is dead.'
• Mary said, 'Jane is dead.'

The words used are identical, but the meanings are very different. In order to encourage children to appreciate the importance of punctuation, teachers need to discuss its use with children when they are writing and when they are rereading their own writing. For some children to get a feel for the pace and length of sentences it can be useful to read *with* them, gently emphasising the punctuation by pauses and voice modulation.

USSR

'Adults who care for children as readers must make sure that children have time to read for themselves.' Aidan Chambers, *The Reading Environment*, Thimble Press (1991).

Many schools devote a regular part of each school day to allow children to spend an extended period reading alone. Some call this USSR (**U**ninterrupted **S**ustained **S**ilent **R**eading). Others call it ERIC (**E**verybody **R**eading **I**n **C**lass). Still others call it SQUIRT (**Shh Qu**iet **I**t's **R**eading **T**ime). But perhaps the most informal is DEAR – **D**rop **E**verything **A**nd **R**ead!

Although it is known by various acronyms, the principle behind the practice remains the same. It provides children with much-needed practice in being readers. In *Extending Beginning Reading*, Vera Southgate revealed that children who were newly fluent readers spent on average no more than two consecutive minutes on reading tasks. This seminal work highlighted the inadequate provision in most classrooms for children to practise the reading they had so carefully been taught. It also drew attention to the fact that it was quite surprising that any children became readers, considering the lack of emphasis upon reading as an activity in the classroom.

Why USSR?

USSR enables children to see the goal of learning to read, that is, the opportunity to take pleasure and information from books. It differs from times spent reading to the teacher, when the emphasis is upon progress and diagnostic assessment; it differs from story-telling and reading aloud sessions, when the emphasis is upon adult mediation. Children have the freedom to choose reading material for the USSR session. They might choose a simple book they can read effortlessly; they might like to look at the pictures of a book that has a very difficult text; they might be reading a comic from home; they might choose to read a hobby magazine.

All this variety of reading encourages children to become discriminating readers. They begin to develop their own tastes in reading material, and these preferences are what will keep children interested in reading long after the cosy world of the early years classroom has been left far behind.

How to set up USSR in the infant classroom

Uninterrupted...
This reading time is for all children, irrespective of their reading capabilities. To ensure that interruptions are few and far between, it is a good idea to allow children time to choose the books they think they will need to keep themselves interested for the duration of the session. This minimises the occasions when children walk around the classroom, distracting other young readers. It can also provide the teacher with some interesting information about children's attitude to and experience with books. Some inexperienced readers can hardly stagger away from the book corner with the pile of books they think they will need to keep them occupied for a ten-minute quiet reading time. Observation of children's reading habits provides valuable information for the profiles of young readers.

The teacher should also be engaged in a reading task during USSR. This may provide the opportunity for the teacher to read some children's books with which she is unfamiliar; or she may choose to bring her own book from home to read. One class teacher reluctantly accepted this advice and brought his own book into the classroom to read. At first he found there were too many distractions to allow him to become engrossed in his book. However, after a short time, he

became completely absorbed in what he was reading and the next thing he knew was that all the children were around his desk shouting at him, telling him that they should be in the hall for indoor games. At first he felt ashamed that he had been so involved with his own reading that he had become deaf to the cries of the class, but on reflection he realised that he had provided the children with the perfect role model of an adult who was so swept up in the world of a book that even twenty-eight shouting children could not bring him back to reality! That is a lesson too few children have the opportunity of witnessing.

Sustained...
Many teachers shy away from introducing quiet reading in the infant years, fearing that the children will lack the stamina to persist at a reading activity without adult support. It is best to start by aiming for approximately five minutes of reasonable quiet. For some classes this is a major achievement. Once the children have shown that they can cope with a short period of reading, the teacher can gradually extend the session to approximately 15 minutes.

Silent...
Obviously in the infant classroom there is unlikely to be absolute silence. Even if every child is engrossed in what he or she is reading there is still likely to be a murmur of noise from those readers who still derive pleasure from vocalising as they read. Other children enjoy pointing out details from their book to their neighbours and, provided this is kept 'on task', it would be pointless to forbid such spontaneous responses to the text. Indeed, if no child responded in this way, one would have to question the quality of the books they were reading. Good books demand a response and young readers need the reassurance of sharing that response.

Reading...
Of course, in the infant classroom there are going to be some children who are still having considerable difficulties in decoding print. For such children, USSR is *reading* only in so far as they behave like readers, namely by choosing books, turning pages and looking at pictures. However, we must not underestimate the importance of these reading behaviours in the child's developing perception of what it is to be a reader. Going through the motions of being a reader is one of the vital preparatory experiences before gaining mastery over decoding.

When children are offered time to become familiar not only with reading but also with books, there is a great benefit to their understanding of the reading process. Reading is no longer competitive or dependent upon the teacher's choice. USSR is not just a perk for those readers able to read

competently, but it also offers the opportunity for all children to discover the pleasures of books.

Some questions about USSR

Should the whole school be doing USSR at the same time?

This approach can be very useful for eight- to eleven-year-olds, when a great majority of them will be making good progress towards fluent reading. However, for four- to seven-year-olds it might not be practical for the whole school to have a simultaneous quiet reading time. It is perfectly reasonable for different classes to arrange to do quiet reading at different times. The biggest advantage of it being a whole-school activity is that one is less likely to use the time for other things. If your children are up to their elbows in paint just as quiet reading time approaches you are far less likely to suggest that everyone gets cleaned up for reading if only your class is going to do it. If, however, you know that the rest of the school is going to be very quiet and that the noise of your children will be very obvious you are more likely to make the effort to get cleaned up.

Should USSR take place every day?

The purpose of USSR is to give all children an extended time in which to engage in the task of being a reader. Whilst this does not have to happen every day, it certainly should happen at least three times a week. One possible way to fit this into the already crowded timetable might be to alternate the quiet reading sessions with teacher-led reading sessions during which the teacher reads to the class some of the books available for their USSR choice. These sessions might then enable children to feel they could cope with such books on their own during a quiet reading session.

Yet another alternative would be to have three USSR sessions per week and on the intervening days have short book talks or book awareness sessions with the class. Activities for these sessions might include:
• encouraging children to bring books from home;
• teachers bringing in all the things they have read over the past few days to show the variety of things that form one's reading experience;
• looking at several books by the same author or illustrator, talking about the illustration styles and so on;
• talking about books serialised on television and books written as a spin-off from TV programmes.

All of these activities help to focus children's minds upon what it is to be a reader, namely to hold views and

opinions about what one reads, to have certain expectations about different books and to enjoy sharing reading experiences with others.

What books are needed for USSR?

There is no need to have a special supply of books available solely for USSR sessions. All the books in the classroom should be available for USSR and it is important that in USSR sessions children have considerable scope for choice. Obviously when a child reads to the teacher much of the reading material will be gently guided by her. Mostly it

will consist of books that the child will be able to read with some success. However, in USSR children should have the opportunity both to romp through 'simple' books and to look at the pictures of more 'difficult' books. Both of these activities can give children pleasure in reading.

Should I allow children time to choose books before the USSR session begins?

The advantage of doing this is that it reduces the movement of children around the classroom, which is always a potential distraction for others. As they become independent readers, many children will be happy to select one book for the duration of the quiet reading session. Others will spend several sessions reading

through a longer text. Children with less reading stamina may need two or three books to entertain them over a 15-minute session.

What should the teacher do during USSR?

This is neither a time for hearing children read nor for preparing the paint pots for the art lesson! If children see that you do not think it important enough to stop everything and read, the status of reading will be lowered in their eyes. It might seem to be a waste of your extremely busy time just to sit and read. Indeed, it may seem to be failing to teach children which, after all, is what you are paid to do! However, it is a fact that most children have no role model of adults reading. They perceive reading as something that adults tell them to do but which adults, including teachers, rarely do themselves. Unless children can see reading as part and parcel of adult life, many will not see the purpose of it in their own lives and will not feel inspired to continue with it.

ACTIVITIES

1. Book record

Age range
Five to six.

Group size
Individuals.

What you need
Paper, pen.

What to do
Keep a careful record of the books the child chooses to read. This record will reveal the child's preferences. It may become apparent that the child chooses only one type of text, for example, fiction or non-fiction, or only selects one subject, for example horses, Dracula or reading scheme books. Some older children may choose only one author, for example, Roald Dahl or Sheila McCullogh.

By recording this information you will be alerted to the child who is selecting too exclusively. It may be appropriate to introduce this reader to other topics, authors and genres.

2. Chart of reading experience

Age range
Six to eight.

Group size
Individuals.

What you need
Copies of photocopiable page 176, pen.

What to do
Use photocopiable page 176 to keep a record of the types of text that the child chooses to read. This chart complements

How to choose a story book

1. Look at the cover. Does the book look *interesting*?

2. Look at the author's *name*. Have you read other books by this author?

3. Look at the *front* cover or the back of the book. You will find a short description of what happens in the book.

4. Read *one* page. Can you read most of the words without much difficulty?

5. *Read* the book by flicking through the pages. Does it look like the kind of book you enjoy reading?

...ake your decision

Clean hands please!

INFORM

FIRE

Class 4's POEMS

Down the Far

The Ruined Castle

I've got Measles

I am an Elephant

Suzy goes Swim...

Julie and the Dragon

the book record, but may be more useful for the older fluent reader. It will enable you quickly to identify a child's range of reading experience and ensure that all types of text are offered to the reader.

3. Choosing a story book

Age range
Six to eight.

Group size
Individuals.

What you need
Copies of photocopiable page 177.

What to do
Give the children copies of photocopiable page 177 and ask them to use the sheet each time they choose a book from the book corner.

Introduce the concept of acronyms and explain that each letter of the word INFORM stands for a point they must consider when choosing a book.

Alternatively enlarge the chart and use it as a poster to be referred to when a child is uncertain what to choose next.

4. Selecting information books

Age range
Six to eight.

Group size
Whole class.

What you need
Copy of photocopiable page 178, felt-tipped pens, pencils.

What to do
Enlarge photocopiable page 178 and allow a small group of children to decorate it. Explain the concept of a flow chart and show the children how it works.

CHAPTER 11

Using books across the curriculum

Both fiction and non-fiction books play an important part in any topic or project. However, although the division into fiction and non-fiction is generally easy for adults to recognise, for young children this is far from the case. Children believe in fairy tales, Father Christmas, giants and monsters for a long time, and teachers need constantly to draw children's attention to the difference between a story book and the reference books they are using.

BACKGROUND

Using fiction to support a topic

Many topics are chosen precisely because the school is well resourced in the appropriate books. Generally these are non-fiction books, chosen either because they have a simple and informative text or because the illustrations are of such outstanding quality that the teacher can use them, even if the children are unlikely to be able to read the text, or because of a combination of the two factors. Fiction books are generally read aloud to the class and are only included if they support the topic. Many topics are universal in appeal because they match the needs and interests of the young child. Such topics include 'Myself', 'My school', 'Where we live' and 'Dinosaurs'.

The following list of fiction books could be used to support these topics and to offer children situations and experiences that enable them to relate to the topics in a more personal way.

Myself

Dalgliesh, A. (1973) *The Bears of Hemlock Mountain*, Young Puffin.
Edwards, D. (1969) *My Naughty Little Sister*, Methuen/Mammoth.
Hoban, R. (1983) *Bedtime for Frances*, Hippo.
Hughes, S. (1975) *Helpers*, Bodley Head/Armada Lions.
Keller, H. (1987) *Lizzie's Invitation*, Julia Macrae/Walker.

Murphy, J. (1982) *Peace at Last*, Macmillan/Picturemac.

My school

Giff, P.R. (1989) *Today was a Terrible Day*, Kestrel/Picture Puffin.
Uttley, A. (1986) *Fuzzypeg Goes to School*, Collins.
Wells, R. (1983) *Timothy Goes to School*, Viking Kestrel/Picture Puffin.

Where we live

Gray, N. and Foreman, M. (1985) *I'll Take you to Mrs Cole*, Anderson Press/Picturemac.
Hedderwick, M. (1986) *Katie Morag Delivers the Mail*, Bodley Head.

Dinosaurs

Arkle, P. (1979) *The Village Dinosaur*, Puffin.
Piers, H. (1984) *Long Neck and Thunder Foot*, Picture Puffin.

Using fiction as the basis for a topic

It is also possible to use fiction as a 'launching-pad' for a topic or as the focal point of a cross-curricular topic. This is less common, but it does ensure that all the children have a common point of reference. Obviously, it would be disastrous to 'do a book to death', but young children especially like to relate to a character or incident and this

That giant's not **BIG** enough!

can enable them to understand the different aspects of a topic more easily.

For a book to be used as a 'launching pad', it is essential that the children are really familiar with the story. This means that the book should have been read and discussed on several occasions. If there are many characters or incidents, some children may find remembering the names and the order of events very difficult. It is only after many hearings that these can get sorted out.

The activities suggested in this chapter are generally suitable for pairs, groups or even the whole class. This enables a teacher to plan for a wide range of different kinds of groups – friends, boys, girls, different ages, different sizes, ability-based groups, boisterous groups, shy groups and mixed ability groups. This variety should give all the children an opportunity to interact and learn from each other.

Younger children may gain more from talking and listening activities, as opposed to reading and writing. It is certainly not envisaged that all

children should attempt to undertake all activities. However, by showing them how knowledge is linked across the curriculum rather than compartmentalised, that you will eventually enable children to seek solutions actively from a variety of viewpoints.

Setting the scene

When introducing the story, start by showing the children the picture and title on the cover of the book. Ask them to imagine what the book may be about. If possible, show them the blurb and discuss with them how this might help them to choose books in the future.

Reading the story

Read the story to the children first without showing them the illustrations, otherwise they might not concentrate on the story but become absorbed in the pictures and lose the story-line. If they have been shown the cover of a book they should

already have some clue to the contents. Let them visualise for themselves the incidents in the story. While reading the story, stop occasionally and ask the children to predict what will happen next. Praise their ideas so long as they make logical sense.

Read the story a second time, showing the children the illustrations. Talk about how the artist interpreted the events. Encourage them to be critical and reflective about how their ideas differ from or complement those of the artist.

Using the book

Select a few activities to extend the book into other areas of the curriculum. If possible, divide the class into groups and suggest different activities according to the needs of a particular group.

ACTIVITIES

Arthur

This very popular story by Amanda Graham (Picture Puffin) concerns a dog in a pet shop. At the end of the day he is the only dog not sold. He notices how popular different animals are and each night he endeavours to become like them. However, each day he is left unsold, until one day a small girl and her Grandpa ask to buy the 'dog who does tricks'.

1. Art

Age range
Five to seven.

Group size
Pairs and the whole class.

What you need
A variety of drawing materials (crayons, charcoal, paints, pencils), large sheets of paper, old magazines, comics and calendars with pictures of dogs and other animals.

What to do
Invite the children to talk about any dogs they have known. What are their different features? Encourage them to describe the dogs using as many different attributes as possible, such as size, length of fur, ears and tail, markings and colour.

Let each child choose a picture of a dog and encourage them to make other comparisons between the dog in the picture and the other dogs they have seen. For example, they may have different noses or whiskers. Divide the group into pairs and explain that one child in each pair is going to draw a dog pretending to be another animal while the other child draws that animal. This does not necessarily have to be an animal from the story. Encourage them to discuss the characteristics of the 'real' animal and how their 'Arthur' can try to become like the animal.

Ask the pairs to look for suitable reference material among the animal pictures. Let the children decide on the medium for their drawings, then let them make their pictures on large sheets of paper. Ask each pair to write a sentence about their animal and how 'Arthur' decided to become this animal.

Collect all the paintings together and make them into a big book or display them on the walls. A cover could be made using the animal pictures cut out of the magazines and calendars.

2. Maths

Age range
Six to seven.

Group size
Four to six children.

What you need
Two or three copies of *Arthur*, copies of photocopiable page 179, pencils, felt-tipped pens, paper, adhesive, coloured card, scissors, thread.

What to do

Counting and recording
Ask the children to look through the book at the different animals Mrs Humbert kept in her pet shop.

Distribute copies of photocopiable page 179 to each group and ask the children to make a list of these animals down the left-hand side. Ask them to write in the second column how many animals of each type they think Mrs Humbert would have had in her shop, or let them try to count the number from the book. Let them use the third column to write down what sort of food she would have to buy for each pet. In the last column, encourage the children to guess how much Mrs Humbert would spend on each animal's food.

If the children are able, let them add up this column and write down how much Mrs Humbert has to spend each day, each week and each month.

Sorting
Get the children to try to sort the animals into sets according to common attributes, such as animals with fur, water animals, climbers, and so on.

Let each group of children choose one of the sets and draw pictures of all the animals within that set. Let them make mobiles by sticking their pictures on to different shapes cut from coloured card so that all the animals from one set are on pieces of card of the same shape and colour. For example, all the birds could be on blue circles.

3. History

Age range
Five to seven.

Group size
The whole class.

What you need
Writing and drawing equipment.

What to do
Discuss with the class how the story talks about time. Day time is when Arthur is trying to attract attention and night time is when he practises being like the different animals. Draw

attention to the passing of time in the story. How long do the children think Arthur was in the pet shop?

Talk about age. How old do they think Mrs Humbert is? How old is Melanie's grandpa? How much older is he than Melanie? Can the children ask their grandparents or an elderly person what it was like when they went to school?

Divide the class into pairs and ask them to plan a day for Arthur. Ask them to consider the following questions:
• When would they feed him?
• When would they take him for a walk?
• What obedience training do they think he would need?
• What time do they think the shop would shut?
• What time should Arthur go to sleep?

Let the children decide how they would like to present this information to the rest of the class. For example, they might choose writing, drawing, drama or diagrams.

The Very Hungry Caterpillar

This book by Eric Carle (Picture Puffin) illustrates the life cycle of a butterfly and provides simple counting experience, listing all the things the caterpillar eats.

1. Science

Age range
Five to six.

Group size
The whole class, working as individuals.

What you need
A copy of *Caterpillar Diary* (Kingscourt Publications), white card, pencils, scissors, felt-tipped pens, paper-fasteners.

What to do
Discuss the life cycle of the butterfly with the children and show them *Caterpillar Diary* (Kingscourt Publications).

Help the children to make time discs showing the life cycle of the butterfly. Cut out two circles of card for each child and use a pencil to draw quarter segments on one circle

Figure 1

as in Figure 1. Ask the children to draw the following pictures on each segment:
• an egg on a leaf;
• a caterpillar;
• a cocoon;
• a butterfly.

Cut a quarter segment out of the second piece of card and fix it over the first piece using a paper-fastener as in Figure 2.

Show the children how to rotate the top piece of card to reveal each illustrated section in turn as you discuss the life cycle.

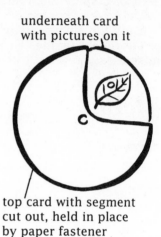

underneath card with pictures on it

top card with segment cut out, held in place by paper fastener

Figure 2

2. Maths

Age range
Five to six.

Group size
The whole class.

What you need
No special equipment.

What to do
Encourage the children to count the number of items that the Very Hungry Caterpillar ate on each day of the week. How

many things did he eat on Saturday? How many days did he spend eating?

3. English

Age range
Five to six.

Group size
Whole class, working as individuals.

What you need
Pencils, paper, poetry books.

What to do
Read the children poems about caterpillars, such as 'The Caterpillar' by Christina Rossetti in *The Book of a Thousand Poems* (Unwin Hyman) or 'Little Arabella Miller' in *This Little Puffin* edited by Elizabeth Matterson (Puffin). Encourage the children to write and illustrate their own caterpillar rhymes.

The Sandal

This book by Philippe Dupasquier (Andersen Press) links Roman times, the present and the future with the theme of a child losing a sandal which is found many years later by another child.

1. English and history

Age range
Six to seven.

Group size
The whole class.

What you need
No special equipment.

What to do
Ask the children what they think it would have been like to live in Roman times. Would it have been very different from now? What do they think life was like for Roman children? Encourage them to use the pictures in the book to find some answers.

Ask the children what they think life will be like in the future. What things of our time do they think ought to be put in a museum for people of the future?

2. Science and technology

Age range
Six to seven.

Group size
The whole class, working individually or in pairs.

What you need
Paper, felt-tipped pens, pencils, construction kits.

What to do
As a class, discuss what is in the picture of the city of today, but not in the pictures of the city in Roman times or in the future. Discuss how various objects have changed. Consider the three kinds of travel shown in the book:
• by foot;
• by car;
• by spaceship.

Ask the children to form pairs to think of ideas for travel in the future. Let them

make designs for vehicles, then try to build them using construction kits.

3. Geography

Age range
Six to seven.

Group size
Pairs.

What you need
Pencils, copies of photocopiable page 180.

What to do
Give each child a copy of photocopiable page 180 and ask them to 'hide' the three sandals somewhere on the grid.

Let the children work with partners, taking it in turns to guess where the other child has hidden the sandals. Encourage them to use grid references when making their guesses and to fill in the square each time they guess.

The winner is the first child to find the location of all three sandals.

The Owl Who Was Afraid of the Dark

This book by Jill Tomlinson (Puffin) tells the story of a baby barn owl who is frightened of the dark, but, through encounters with various people and animals, comes to understand that darkness has many varied qualities, all of which make it an ideal environment for an owl.

1. Science

Age range
Seven to eight.

Group size
The whole class, working individually.

What you need
Reference books about astronomy and about nocturnal animals.

What to do
Discuss the concept of day and night with the children. Can they think of any nocturnal animals? Have they ever seen any? Ask them to research into the subject and report back to the class with their findings.

Use the opportunity to introduce the children to basic astronomy. Encourage the children to ask their parents to take them out on a clear night to look at stars.

2. English

Age range
Seven to eight.

Group size
Pairs.

What you need
Paper, pencils, felt-tipped pens.

What to do
Ask the children to work in pairs to create poems using the following formula:
Light is exciting when...
Dark is exciting when...
Light is kind when...
Dark is kind when...
Light is fun when...
Dark is fun when...
Light is necessary when...

Dark is necessary when...
Light is fascinating when ...
Dark is fascinating when...
Light is wonderful when...
Dark is wonderful when...
Light is beautiful when...
Dark is beautiful when....

Encourage the children to write out their poems within decorative borders.

3. Technology

Age range
Seven to eight.

Group size
Pairs.

What you need
Small soft toys, polythene bags, fabric scraps, scissors, thread, pencils, paper.

What to do
Ask the children to work in pairs to design a parachute to help Plop land safely.

Give each pair a soft toy to represent Plop and a range of polythene and fabric scraps to make the parachute.

Ask them to devise a fair system to test the parachutes and to test their results.

Peepo

This picture story book by Janet and Allan Ahlberg (Puffin) shows family life during the Second World War, and is supported by a rhythmic text. The family are shown from a viewpoint that is both that of the baby featured in the story and that of the reader. The detailed illustrations invite close attention and provide a wealth of detailed information about the way some people lived at this time. The rhythm

and repetition encourage listeners and readers to join in.

1. History

Age range
Five to six.

Group size
The whole class, working in pairs.

What you need
Pencils, paper.

What to do
Read the book and show the pictures to the children. Let them look closely at the pictures. Ask them to notice

differences and similarities between the home in the book and their own homes.

Let the children form pairs to discuss their observations, then put each pair with another pair and ask them to compare their ideas.

When the children have talked through their observations, ask a representative from each group to report back to the class. Get them to make a list of their observations under the following headings:
• things that have changed;
• things that are the same;
• things that are new;
• things that are no longer in our homes.

When the list is finished encourage the children to consider why some things change and other things stay the same.

2. Science

Age range
Five to seven.

Group size
The whole class, working in pairs.

What you need
Paper, pencils.

What to do
Give each pair a sheet of paper and ask them to make a list of all the things in their homes that work by electricity.

Let the pairs look at copies of the book and ask them to make a list of things in the book that work by electricity. Display the lists for the children to read and discuss. Ask them why they think that there are more electrical things in our homes now.

3. English – stories and reading

Age range
Five to seven.

Group size
The whole class.

What you need
Paper, pencils, felt-tipped pens.

What to do
Group the children so that they can all see a copy of the book.

Read the book aloud and ask the children to look at the words and pictures as you read.

Ask them to think of any other stories or rhymes that feature some of the scenes, objects or characters shown in the pictures, such as mother making porridge, granny hanging out the washing, making a cup of tea or babies fast asleep. Make a class anthology of their suggestions and let the children illustrate it.

4. English – stories and poems

Age range
Five to seven.

Group size
Whole class.

What you need
Paper, pencils, felt-tipped pens.

Rock-a-bye Baby By

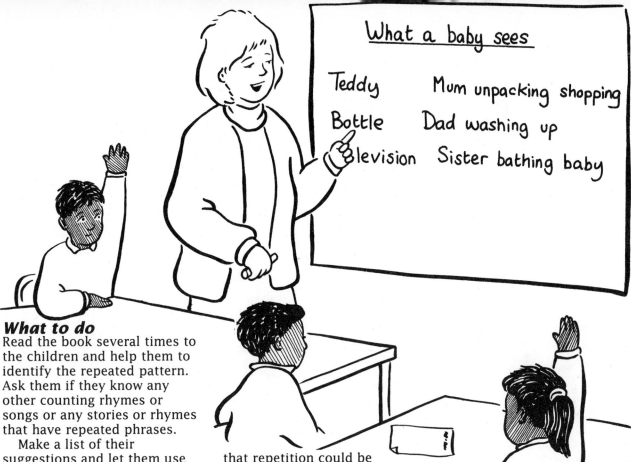

What a baby sees

Teddy   Mum unpacking shopping

Bottle   Dad washing up

Television   Sister bathing baby

What to do

Read the book several times to the children and help them to identify the repeated pattern. Ask them if they know any other counting rhymes or songs or any stories or rhymes that have repeated phrases.

Make a list of their suggestions and let them use this as a basis for making a class counting rhyme book or a collection of stories that use repeated rhymes or phrases to carry the action of the story forward.

5. English – writing together

Age range
Five to seven.

Group size
The whole class.

What you need
Paper, felt-tipped pens, scissors, a word processor (optional), a stapler.

What to do
Read the book to the children, drawing their attention to the repetition in the text. Suggest that repetition could be included in a similar poem that they could all help to write.

Ask the class to suggest some things a baby might see. List their suggestions and discuss with them which ones should be included in their rhyme and in which order the events should occur. Number the events and cross out all the unwanted ideas.

Start writing the first part of the rhyme on a large sheet of paper, saying the words as you write them:

'Here's a little baby
One, two, three...'

Refer the children to the plan and ask them what they would like to add to the verse. When agreement is reached write down the rest of the verse, once again saying the words as you write them. Using the book as a model, continue to develop the story.

When the story is complete,

introduce the idea of making a class book and discuss the format that it should take. If it is decided to use a 'peephole' format, make sure that the pages are square and that the children appreciate the need for their pictures to work out from the centre of the page.

Alternatively a flap format might be used with 'Peepo' written on flaps which would cover each illustration.

Type or write out the story and give the children different parts of the story to illustrate.

Finally, assemble the book and staple it together. Invite the authors and illustrators to read it to themselves, their classmates or in assembly.

The Three Little Pigs

Tony Ross's retelling of this traditional tale (Beaver) adds new dimensions which draw the reader into a battle of wits. For example, although the wolf's demise follows the traditional pattern, other strategies for outwitting him add to the drama of the situation and extend the story. The increasingly energetic illustrations support the mounting tension of the text. The conclusion of the book invites consideration of environmental issues.

1. Science – classifying

Age range
Six to seven.

Group size
The whole class, working in pairs.

What you need
Straw, sticks, bricks or stones, paper, pencils, felt-tipped pens.

What to do
Read the story to the children and encourage them to consider how and why two of the houses succumbed to the wolf's attack.

Following the discussion, explain to the class that they are going to try to decide why the bricks were able to withstand the wolf's attack. Provide the children with some straw, sticks and bricks or stones. If necessary, explain that in some areas stones rather than bricks are used for building.

Ask the children to form pairs and to discuss the properties of each of the materials. Support their discussions by asking questions. Which is the hardest? Which is the softest? Can any of the objects be squeezed or stretched? When the children have decided about the properties of each of the materials, ask them to think of other objects which have similar properties.

Discuss with the children how they might best present their information for others to read. Is it possible to draw or write about it? Could they draw a chart or table? What about a diagram?

When each presentation is finished make a display of them and ask the class to read them all. Finally, discuss with the class which they thought were the most effective presentations and why.

This activity can help children appreciate that reading and writing can take many forms.

2. Science – strength

Age range
Six to seven.

Group size
Groups of four or five.

What you need
Straw, sticks, bricks or stones.

What to do
Provide each group with some straw, sticks and bricks or stones.

Ask the children to design an experiment to test the strength of the three types of material. Help the children consider the problem by asking them the following questions.

• How easy is it to bend the objects?
• Can you scratch one thing with either of the others?
• Which is the hardest?

When they have all tested their materials, bring the groups together and ask one spokesperson from each group to report on their tests.

3. Mathematics – weight

Age range
Six to seven.

Group size
Pairs.

What you need
Straw, sticks, bricks or stones, scales, paper, pencils.

What to do
Provide each pair of children with some straw, sticks, bricks or stones and some scales.

Invite the children to handle the material and together estimate:
• how many pieces of straw equal the weight of one stick;
• how many sticks equal the weight of one brick or stone;
• how many grams all the straw weighs;
• how many grams all the sticks weigh;
• how many grams all the bricks or stones weigh.

Ask the children to write down each estimate, then ask them to use the scales to check their predictions and write the accurate weights next to their estimates.

Ask the pairs to review their table of results. Which was the most accurate estimate? Which was the least accurate estimate?

Further activity

Ask the children to estimate how many Unifix cubes weigh 50 grams. How many weigh 100 grams? How many children weigh 50 kilos? How many weigh 100 kilos?

4. Mathematics – sets

Age range
Six to seven.

Group size
The whole class.

What you need
A variety of classroom equipment.

What to do

Read the story to the children. Draw their attention to the sets of three that occur in the story and the common features of each set. For example, although the houses were all different, they all had certain common attributes.

When you feel that the children have a general understanding of common attributes within a set, ask them to help you make a display of sets of three. Talk to the children about the sets of objects they have put on display and ask them to suggest ways in which the sets might be labelled. Remind them of the fact that sets have common features and in order to belong to a set each object must possess those features. Suggest various attributes for the sets, such as colour or number of sides. Demonstrate how a label might be written. For example: 'This is a set of

This is a set of three children. They all have red tops.

three books. They all have covers and pages.'

Ask some children to write the labels, or write the labels for them.

5. English – story knowledge

Age range
Six to seven.

Group size
The whole class.

What you need
Different versions of 'The Three Little Pigs', display materials.

What to do

Collect and display different versions of 'The Three Little Pigs'. Read these stories to the children and draw their attention to the similarities and differences in them. Explain that stories used to be told rather than read and that sometimes the story-teller would adapt them to reflect local incidents or conditions. Talk about the language variation in the stories and ask the children why they think the language varies. Ask them if there are any particular language features that appear in most or all of the stories. These might include 'Once upon a time' or 'Long ago'. Why do they think stories and story-tellers use this kind of language?

Ask the children to think of other stories that feature groups of three. Make a collection of these. (It might be interesting to ask why the children think the number three features so frequently in stories.)

6. English – drama

Age range
Five to seven.

Group size
Groups of four.

What you need
Paper, pencils, scissors, felt, fabric scraps, adhesive, wooden spoons.

What to do
Group the children in fours and ask them to draw the faces of the three pigs and the wolf in order to make templates for puppet faces. Help them to make four puppets from felt and fabric scraps stuck on to the bowl of a wooden spoon as shown in the illustration.

When the puppets are finished, give each group a set amount of time to prepare a play about the Three Little Pigs. Invite the groups to perform their plays to the class.

Titch

In this story by Pat Hutchins (Picture Puffin), Titch is the youngest and smallest member of the family. Everything his brother and sister do is bigger and better than anything Titch does. However, one day Titch plants a tiny seed. The seed grows and grows and grows. This is a very simple story but with strong undercurrents that so many children are able to recognise.

1. English

Age range
Four to seven.

Group size
The whole class.

What you need
Card, pens, catalogues or magazines, scissors, adhesive, drawing materials.

What to do
Read the story to the class. Spontaneous comments will arise, with nearly all the children talking about what it is like to live in a world where so many people are so much bigger than they are! This can naturally lead on to a writing activity, if you collect all these comments and write them on to large pieces of card. This in turn can be easily made into a 'big book' which the children might like to illustrate with drawings or by cutting out pictures from magazines or catalogues. Encourage the children to think of other creatures or objects which grow or develop unexpectedly (for example, tadpoles, caterpillars, bulbs, cakes or bread).

Let them use *Titch* as a model for writing their own story. Perhaps they would like to make up a story about the smallest puppy or kitten. How does this pet solve the problem of being the smallest?

How can they find out if they are right? What factors will have to be considered? What if someone has a great deal of puff compared to the others and makes more noise with the recorder than the trumpet?

2. Maths – language

Age range
Four to five.

Group size
The whole class.

What you need
A collection of musical instruments, such as a drum, a trumpet and a recorder.

What to do
Use *Titch* to introduce language associated with mathematical concepts (in, on, beside, larger, smaller).

Show the children a collection of musical instruments and ask them to estimate which is:
• the heaviest;
• the longest;
• the loudest.

3. Maths – time

Age range
Four to six.

Group size
The whole class.

What you need
A ramp or PE bench and box, a collection of wheels of different sizes, a stop-watch.

What to do
Discuss how Pete had a big bike with large wheels, Mary had a bike with middle-sized wheels but Titch had a tiny bike with the smallest wheels.

Ask the children to find three different sized wheels. Make a slope for the wheels to

travel down, using a ramp or a PE bench and a box. Get one child to release the large wheel while another child times with a stop-watch how long it takes for the wheel to reach the finishing line. Let another pair time the middle-sized wheel and a third pair time the smallest wheel. Ask questions such as the following:
• Which wheel went the fastest?
• Which was the slowest?
• Did any of the wheels fall over?
• What size would you like the wheels on your bike to be?

4. Science – classification

Age range
Four to seven.

Group size
The whole class, working in pairs.

What you need
Polythene bags, white card, pencils, paper.

What to do
Take the children for a walk round the school grounds during late summer or autumn and ask them to collect as many seeds as they can find

and to put them into separate polythene bags. Back in the classroom, ask the children to form pairs and give each pair a large piece of white card. Put a few seeds from the collection on to each piece of card so that they are clearly visible. Talk about the different sizes, colours, shapes, smells and textures. Get the children to classify the seeds. Explain that some seeds will belong to more than one category. Let the children count the number of seeds in each category, then record their findings. Ask the whole class to compare their results.

5. Science – change

Age range
Five to seven.

Group size
The whole class, working in pairs.

What you need
A variety of seeds, paper, an adhesive stick, bowls of water.

What to do
Give each pair of children a piece of paper and ask them to select four types of seeds and to take four samples of each type. Use an adhesive stick to draw a line down the left-hand side of the sheet, then get the children to put *two* of each seed carefully on to the line. Soak the remaining seeds in water overnight.

The following day, give the children their soaked seeds and ask them if they notice any changes.

Let them draw another line of adhesive down the page and place two more of each seed opposite their original seeds. What do they notice? Have the seeds got any larger? Discuss with the children the need for seeds to have water in order to grow.

6. Science – recording

Age range
Five to seven.

Group size
The whole class, working in pairs.

What you need
A saucer, blotting paper, water, cress seeds, paper, a ruler.

What to do
Soak some cress seeds overnight.

Give each pair of children a saucer with damp blotting paper in it, then let the children scatter the cress seeds over the paper. Ask them to put the saucers in different places around the classroom.

Tell the children that it is very important that the paper is not allowed to dry out, but that if there is too much water the seed will rot.

Let the children keep a daily diary in which they must record all the things they notice about the seeds and also describe what they did. They should describe where their cress is, for example, on the window-sill. Do the seeds get enough sun? Do some seeds get more than others?

After a week, compare the different saucers. Can the children think why some seeds have not grown as much as others? Let them compare their diaries to see whether different things were done. Let them measure the cress to see which has grown the tallest.

The children may like to make a class book in which they describe what they have done and write in extracts from their diary. Discuss with them the features of a non-fiction book. The book could contain a contents page, some charts and an index.

7. Music

Age range
Four to seven.

Group size
The whole class.

What you need
No special equipment.

What to do
Teach the children the tune of 'Here we go round the mulberry bush' but substitute lines which describe how to plant and grow a seed. For example:

This is the way we plant our seed, plant our seed, plant our seed.
This is the way we plant our seed on a bright and sunny morning.

This is the way we water our seed, water our seed, water our seed.
This is the way we water our seed on a bright and sunny morning.

This is how much our seed has grown, seed has grown, seed has grown.
This is how much our seed has grown on a bright and sunny morning.

Our seed has grown a seed of its own, seed of its own, seed of its own.
Our seed has grown a seed of its own on a bright and sunny morning.

This is the way we plant our seed, etc.

Further activity
Help the children to make up an action counting song based on a seed growing. Ask the children to make their hands into fists and, as they describe each seed being planted, encourage them to point down with a finger. When the tenth seed is planted let them wriggle their fingers and turn their hands over to show how the seeds grew up through the soil and peeped through the earth. For example, they could say:

One little seed was planted deep,
We left it there to sleep, sleep, sleep.

Two little seeds were planted deep,
We left them there to sleep, sleep, sleep.

Three etc.

Ten little seeds were planted deep,
THEN – out of the ground they all did peep.

CHAPTER 12

The bilingual classroom

'Bilingual children should be considered an advantage in the classroom rather than a problem. The evidence shows that such children will make greater progress in English if they know that their knowledge of their mother tongue is valued, if it is recognised that their experience of language is likely to be greater than that of their monoglot peers and, indeed, if their knowledge and experience can be put to good use in the classroom...' (DES/WO 1989a).

The number of children in our classrooms for whom English is not their first language is steadily increasing and it is imperative that schools consider the needs of these children. Schools must have a clear policy which addresses the needs of these children and which builds upon the strengths of the individual child.

BACKGROUND

How do children learn a second language?

Research was undertaken in 1983 by Krashen and Terrell to try to discover how children learn a second language most effectively. They came to three main conclusions.

• Children learn a new language best when they are not forced to start speaking straight away – they need a silent period.

• The best context is one which places a strong emphasis upon meaningful communication.

• The new language must be used in situations which are relevant and interesting for the learner.

The researchers stressed that the teacher should always use the target language and that the focus of the communication should be on a topic of interest to the child, with the teacher placing understanding by the pupil as the priority. Obviously, with many young children, listening and speaking will have to take place for some considerable time before the teacher can contemplate formal teaching of reading. However, many classroom activities could be concluded by the teacher selecting a relevant phrase or song and showing the child how the words can be represented in print.

For some children the direction of English print (reading from top left to bottom right) and the letter shapes may be different from their own language. Teachers need to be conscious that these conventions have to be highlighted again and again.

A welcoming environment

Acknowledgement of the different languages spoken by pupils can start as soon as the parents or children step on to the school grounds. Notices in different languages, a welcome poster and displays which exhibit the work of the children incorporating the different languages all help to underline the message that the school welcomes all children and parents.

One of the most difficult tasks for schools is to persuade parents that their presence at school meetings is both needed and appreciated. A parent's natural reluctance may be increased if notice of the meetings is only provided in English and the parent finds this very difficult to understand.

Most counties now provide a translation service in the main languages, but some of the less usual languages are more difficult to acquire. Many secondary teachers of modern languages are only too happy to help with European languages and may also be able to identify senior pupils in the school who could help. Evening classes can also provide a source of adults who could help with translations; contact your local adult

International Festival

education institute for advice. Photocopiable page 181 gives a very brief general invitation in Urdu, Greek and Arabic as an example.

Frequently parents and children worry over such things as school dinners, uniform requirements and even the regulations about the time children should be brought to school and collected. A letter describing what is provided and what choice is permitted can alleviate parental concern and help to build up confidence. Some schools have been lucky enough to find a parent who can act as 'go-between' and who enjoys the responsibility of disseminating information from the school and encouraging parents to attend school functions.

In the same way, ensuring the classroom offers familiarity and security can ease the child's entry into school. Do the posters displayed depict many nationalities? Is the children's work displayed around the walls? Have they been encouraged to write in their own language if English is not their mother tongue? If the teacher can welcome the children in their first language as they enter the classroom then a completely different atmosphere is created. One school chose to learn to greet visitors and to say goodbye in a different language each week. Very soon parents began to ask the children every Monday what was the new language and to practise it themselves. Naturally the children became increasingly proud of their knowledge.

An international festival

Schools lucky enough to have children from many cultures are more easily able to hold an international festival. The children should be encouraged to provide the entertainment in the form of singing, dancing, poetry and music, while the parents could be prevailed upon to provide some 'finger' food from their own or another chosen country. (It may be necessary to suggest that each child chooses just three items to sample as this food often proves irresistible to hungry young boys and girls!) National costume will help to make it a more festive occasion and the children could be encouraged to choose any country in the world and dress up as near as possible to the national costume. Visibly welcoming parents and showing them the valuable part they can play in school life helps to establish the strong links that form so vital a part in children's education.

These activities may seem a long way from reading, but if children are happy and comfortable in their school, and real communication takes place between the parent and the school, then the child is much more likely to learn.

Introducing reading

There is no separate technique for introducing reading to children for whom English is a second language, just as there is no one method for children whose only language is English. The same preparation is needed for all children, but bilingual children probably need longer to build up their spoken English so that their

reading can be firmly based upon understanding (see Chapters 1 to 3).

Language acquisition generally follows the same pattern that we observe in toddlers. As the children become more competent in the second language, they use sign language less and less and begin to use short phrases, such as 'there dog' or 'teacher come'. There is a danger that teachers might be so pleased with this communication that they accept it without modelling the more expanded version that parents naturally use. For instance, many parents of two-year-old children hear the same kind of two-word phrases and respond quite naturally with 'Yes, the dog is over there'.

Teachers are naturally anxious to ensure that the children 'catch up' with their peers, and consequently may try to introduce too much too

quickly. Remember that children need to know the conventions of print and understand the terminology of reading, and this needs to be established before embarking on decoding. (See Chapter 3, 'Big books'.) Children need to hear and understand as many stories as possible so that they begin to understand what reading is (see Chapter 1, 'Introducing reading') and they need to recognise the importance of being able to 'read the environment' (see Chapter 2).

As a child gains in confidence, the teacher can begin to share simple meaningful texts, followed up with numerous opportunities for the child to create his own texts. Playing simple games can help to consolidate vocabulary and letter sounds (see Chapter 4, 'Developing a sight vocabulary').

Dual language texts

There is an increasing number of dual language books available and these should form part of every school's book resources. In many cases, the best of the children's books are now being translated into many languages. The resulting books do much to establish the equal status of all languages, and actively encourage literacy in the mother tongue, as well as providing texts which can help to bridge the gap between home and school. One school found dual language books especially valuable for grandparents to read aloud to their grandchildren. This often made the child the focus of attention in the family.

However, just because a book is available in several languages, it is not necessarily 'good'. Just as much care needs to be exercised with the choice of these books as with any other texts. Special care needs to be taken with non-fiction books, as all too often these judge societies in relation to Western standards. People are seen as 'poor' because they do not own Western goods, and all too often non-Western societies are shown as primitive or quaint. When selecting non-fiction books for the classroom, it is essential that they are factually accurate and up to date.

Look carefully at the way the language is used.
• Do the books describe Africans, for example, as living in homes or in huts?
• Do the books represent peoples with a variety of attributes rather than stereotyping whole groups?
• Are the illustrations powerful and informative or are they demeaning caricatures?
• Do the books accurately reflect the population of Britain? This means more than a token black child included in a sprinkling of illustrations. Remember that books should be equally appropriate 'in an all-black classroom and an all-white classroom'. Books which do not fit into this category should be discarded.

Nursery rhymes

Nursery rhymes play a vital part in helping children to acquire language. The following is a Muslim rhyme based on the English 'One, two, buckle my shoe' taken from *Muslim Nursery Rhymes* (The Islamic Foundation).

The straight path
One, two – What I say must be true.
Three, four – My faith must be sure.
Five, six – Try not to play tricks.
Seven, eight – My way must be straight.
Nine, ten – Help women and men.
Eleven, twelve – For truth I must delve.
Thirteen, fourteen – Be tidy and clean.
Fifteen, sixteen – Must never be mean.
Seventeen, eighteen – By Allah I'm seen.
Nineteen, twenty – My provision is plenty.

Recommended dual language texts

The letters after the title refer to the languages available.

A – Arabic
B – Bengali
C – Chinese
G – Greek
H – Hindi
P – Punjabi
Ta – Tamil
Tu – Turkish
U – Urdu
V – Vietnamese

Fiction

Asian Nursery Rhymes and Tapes, (Mantra).
(B.G.H.P.U.)
Ben's Baby, Michael Foreman (Magi).
(B.G.H.P.U.V.)
The Boy Who Cried Wolf, Tony Ross (Magi).
(B.G.H.P.U.V.)
Dear Zoo, Rod Campbell (Ingham Yates).
(B.H.P.U.)
A Four Tongued Alphabet, Ruth Brown (Andersen).
The Hare and the Tortoise, Gabriel Douloubakas (Luzac).
(B.G.H.P.U.)
How Do I Put It On?, Shigeo Watanabe (Bodly Head).
(B.G.H.P.U.V.)
Jambo means Hello (Swahili Alphabet), Muriel Feelings (Pied Piper).
King Jahingir and the Baby, I. Anand (Andre Deutsch).
(A.B.G.H.P.)
Mighty Rabbit, Elizabeth Sharma (Tiger Books).
(B.G.H.P.U.)
Muslim Nursery Rhymes, (Islamic Foundation).
My Favourite Things, 'All About Me' series, J. Ingham/Das Prodeapta (Blackie).
(B.G.P.U.)

The Night The Animals Fought, Jesus Zaton (Mantra).
(B.G.P.U.)
Not Now Bernard, (video available), David McKee (Ingham/Yates).
(B.G.H.P.U.)
The *Spot* books, especially *Where's Spot?*, Eric Hill (Baker Books).
(B.C.G.H.Ta.Tu.U.)
Topiwalo the Hatmaker, Clifford Norgate (cassette available), (Harmony).
(B.G.H.P.U.)

Non-fiction

Duets, B. Dhanjal (Hamish Hamilton).
(B.P.U.)
Let's Talk About..., M. Martinez (Magi).
(B.G.H.P.U.V.C.)
'Starters' series (*Butterflies, Frogs, Milk, Rain*), (Macdonald).
(B.G.P.U.)
'The Terraced House Books' (*My Mum, My School, My Home*, etc) Peter Heaslip (Methuen).
(B.G.P.U.)

ACTIVITIES

1. Stand and deliver

Age range
Any age.

Group size
Two to ten.

What you need
Card, scissors, a pen.

What to do
Before the activity, make a number of flash cards with a selection of commands on them, such as 'sit down'; 'stand up'; 'pick up a book'; 'sit on a chair'; 'sit on a table'; 'put your hand on your head'; 'touch your toes', and so on.

Shuffle the cards and place them face down on the table. Hold up one of the cards so that the group can see it. Depending upon the ability of the children, either read the card out aloud for the group to obey or ask the group to read it and obey the instruction. When all the group have succeeded, read the next card. Continue the game until all the cards have been obeyed.

It is better to repeat the commands so that the children see, hear and become familiar with a few at a time. Then you can gradually add to these. This ensures that the children achieve a higher rate of success, since too many commands at a time can lead to confusion.

As the children become more confident, make the activity into a 'knock-out' game where the last child to do the activity has to be 'out'. Continue this until only one child remains. Obviously this is better with smaller groups as if it takes too long the children will become restless.

As the children become more adept at this game, use instructions that look similar so that the children have to read with greater attention. For example, use all of the following:
• Sit down on a table.
• Sit down under a table.
• Sit down by a table.

2. Snapshots

Age range
Any age.

Group size
Pairs.

What you need
Copies of photocopiable page 182, two identical sets of coloured crayons or felt-tipped pens, a screen.

What to do
Ask the two children to sit together and place a screen between them so that they cannot see what the other child is doing. Give each child a copy of photocopiable page 182.

Ask the children to take it in turns to say what colour they

are using to colour the various articles of clothing. (For example, 'I am colouring the jumper green'; 'I am colouring the shoes red'; 'I am colouring the hair black'...) Ask the other child to colour in the objects using the appropriate colour.

At the end of the activity let the children compare drawings to check that they have a pair of identical twins.

Extend the activity to labelling the different articles of clothing so that each child may choose three items and ask the other child to label them.

Further activity
Let the children take it in turns to instruct each other on making a drawing. For example, 'My monster has a round head'; 'My monster has four eyes on the top of his head'; 'My monster is saying "hello"'.

3. Wrap it up

Age range
Any age.

Group size
Pairs.

What you need
Two identical sheets of wrapping paper with a variety of different pictures on them (such as different animals, different flowers or letters of the alphabet), a large piece of card, adhesive, scissors, a screen, a pen.

What to do
Before the activity, mount both sheets of wrapping paper on to card. Cut one of the sheets into equal squares, the size depending upon the age and ability of the children. For example, a simple game might only have four squares, whereas a more difficult one might have twelve.

Start by demonstrating how to pose the questions and ask the children to try to follow

them. The children will soon be able to play without teacher involvement.

Let the two players sit opposite each other with a screen in between so that they cannot see what the other is doing. Give one child the whole sheet and the other the squares.

Ask the player with the whole sheet to describe for her partner where each card should be placed. (For example, 'The top right-hand corner has an island with two parrots and a monkey on it'.)

When all the cards have been described, let the player with the whole sheet take it round to place beside the second player. Encourage the two players to compare their sheets to see if they are identical.

Extend the activity to pictures, words, phrases and sentences written on to a large sheet of paper with matching cards made for the second player.

Further activity
Give the children strips of paper with pictures, words, phrases or sentences on them and encourage them to instruct each other on the order in

which they should place them.
For example:

First child: 'My first picture is of a red house.'

Second child: 'My first picture is of a red house; my second picture is of a blue balloon.'

Alternatively:

First child: 'My first sentence says, "I am going to catch a bus." '

Second child: 'My first sentence says, "I am going to catch a bus"; my second sentence says "I am going to buy some apples." '

Each child should repeat the previous sentences before adding the next.

4. Alphabet frieze

Age range
Any age.

Group size
The whole class.

What you need
An alphabet book, alphabet stencils, pens, pencils, card, scissors, old magazines and catalogues, adhesive, a copy of *Jambo Means Hello* by Muriel Feelings (optional).

What to do
Show the children the alphabet book and discuss with them the alphabet order. Explain that they are going to make an

alphabet frieze for the classroom wall.

Let each of the children choose a letter and ask them to suggest something that they know and like that illustrates the initial sound of their letter. (It may be necessary to allocate some of the more unusual letters to the more confident children.) Give each child the stencil for their letter and a piece of card and explain that they should trace the letter either at the top or bottom of the card.

Let the children choose whether to draw a picture for their letter or to cut out and stick on a picture from a magazine or catalogue. Encourage the children to write the name of their object in English and/or their own language.

Display the alphabet frieze along the classroom wall.

Further activity
Show the children the book *Jambo Means Hello* by Muriel Feelings, in which the author has taken a word in Swahili for each letter of the alphabet and given its English translation.

Ask the children to ask their parents if they know any words from any foreign languages. This new collection of words could be used to make a multilingual alphabet. (With languages that use scripts other than Roman, parents might be able to provide both the original script and a phonic translation.)

5. Connections

Age range
Six and upwards.

Group size
Two to four.

What you need
Old magazines and catalogues, scissors, paper, pencils.

What to do
Cut out pictures of people, objects and places from magazines. Show all the

My name is Daniel.

My favourite food is chocolate cake.

My best friend is Tom.

I can speak French and English.

My favourite game is football.

Look at us!

pictures to the children and ensure they can recognise them. Ask each child in turn to choose any two pictures and to make a connection between the two they have chosen. (For example, 'I like ice-cream and apples.') Return the pictures to the pile and let another child choose any two to make a connection.

As the children become more confident, select the two pictures yourself and ask the children to try to make a connection.

Make flash card strips with a name of each object, person or place written on them for the children to match to the appropriate picture. Finally, ask the children to work in pairs and write a sentence connecting any two of the labelled photographs. Ask them to read their sentence to the others in the group.

6. Look at me!

Age range
Any age.

Group size
Any size.

What you need
A camera that can take close-ups, film, card, pencils.

What to do
Take an individual photograph of each child in the group and mount these pictures on to card.

Discuss with the group all the things they would like to learn about each other, such as their favourite food, their best present, their best friend, what languages they can speak, their favourite game, their favourite television programme, the pet they would like to have, and so on.

Write on the card below the photograph the statements that result from this discussion and let each child complete their own 'identikit'.

Mount these cards on the classroom wall for all the children to read.

7. Sing along

Age range
Any age.

Group size
The whole class.

What you need
A board and markers or chalks, pieces of card, coloured pens, numbers one to ten in as many languages as possible.

What to do
Choose any simple counting rhyme and say it with the children, using the numbers from any of the languages

spoken by the children in the class. Get all the children to join in and learn to count up to five or ten in the different languages.

Write the verse on the board, with the numbers in the script of the chosen language, and show the children what they are singing.

Make number cards for the numbers up to ten in the various languages. Draw the number and write its name on to the card. Hold up the appropriate card as the class sing the songs, or ask a child to hold up the cards.

Mount the cards around the classroom wall when the activity is over.

Examples

• Five little froggies sitting on a well,
One looked up and down he fell.
Four little froggies sitting on a well,
One looked up and down he fell....
(Let the children hold up their hands and, as each frog falls down, bend over one finger.)

• One, two, three, four, five,
Once I caught a fish alive.

Six, seven, eight, nine, ten,
Then I let him go again.

• One potato, two potato, three potato, four;
Five potato, six potato, seven potato, more.

• Two, four, six, eight,
Johnny saw a rattlesnake,
Eating cake by a lake
Two, four, six, eight.

• One little elephant went out one day
Upon a spider's web to play.
He had such tremendous fun
He sent for another elephant to come.
Two little elephants went out one day
Upon a spider's web to play.
They had such tremendous fun
They sent for another elephant to come....

This last rhyme can be played as a game in which the first 'elephant' walks around the room swinging his arm like a trunk. At the end of the verse he chooses a friend who holds on to him with her 'trunk'. This continues until all the children are elephants or until your voice and patience run out!

Further activity
Choose songs that have actions to go with them, and translate certain words. For example, if the children sing 'This is the way we clean our teeth', ask them to sing the verse with the word for 'teeth' translated into another language. Don't forget to tell the children how clever they are!

CHAPTER 13

Supporting the late bloomer

Many teachers feel that if only they could keep certain Y2 children for one more year they would be able to ensure that the child would enter Y3 as a competent reader. Often these are the summer birthday children, but they are rarely given the privilege of having this extra year. They can be described as 'late bloomers' because teachers feel that they are so near to competence in reading that with encouragement and enthusiasm they will blossom fully. However, many teachers also suspect that the long summer holidays and the rather tenuous hold these children have upon reading could mean that they are likely to become struggling readers as they go up the school.

The task of the teacher in Y2 is to try to consolidate the child's reading strategies and to check that he has not become muddled or confused about the goals that are essential in becoming a reader. Above all, the teacher needs to ensure that the child seeks for information and understanding in all that he reads.

BACKGROUND

In some instances the teacher may have inadvertently overemphasised her pleasure when a child appeared to apply a 'good' strategy, with the result that the child then offered this on every occasion. An extreme example of this occurred with a little girl who came across the word 'woodcutter' in her book and quite understandably hesitated. She then said, 'Oh, I can make it into smaller words' and covered over 'cutter' with her thumb. The teacher was very pleased and praised her loudly, especially as she then managed 'woodcutter'. However, the next day the child again hesitated, this time before the word 'window' and immediately she placed her thumb over 'ndow'. Realising this was not helping her, she then put her left thumb over 'win' and her right thumb over the second 'w' exposing 'do' which she proudly read. In a following discussion with the teacher she said, 'You said I could make little words'. What was a good strategy in some instances, coupled with the justified praise she had received, had led her to believe that finding small words would give her access to *all* long words.

Far more frequently, children have been praised for trying to tackle unknown words by sounding out all the letters and have then thought that the way to please the teacher is to do this on every occasion – sometimes even to words that they can recognise!

Others have realised that the illustrations provide a story framework, and these children may offer a good retelling of the book without apparently looking at the words. Was this due to the message they picked up when in the early stages, we suggested that they 'look at the picture'? Perhaps the most difficult 'late bloomer' to recognise is the one who can say all the words correctly but is not processing the meaning within the words so that when the teacher makes a comment or asks what the reader would have done in a similar situation the child looks completely blank.

Many of our 'late bloomers' seem to have confused ideas about what the adult really wants them to achieve. It is worth taking time to see if this is the case. Teachers must ensure that by the time a child is seven he has a clear idea of what reading is: that is, that the words on the page have

Up popped hippo!

Where is Hippo!

something of importance to say to the reader. It may seem frustratingly slow spending time going over all the preparatory work this involves, but if a child leaves Y2 without being secure in this knowledge, his chances of future success are very slim.

How to help

It is worth checking periodically that the child understands the conventions of print and the terminology that the teacher is using. One child was asked to point to the place where he would like the teacher to start reading and to run his finger under the words for her to read. This he did with apparent confidence and accuracy with the text on the left hand page, but the teacher was devastated to see him then use his right index finger and to run this under the text from right to left on the right hand page! Similarly, some seven-year-olds were shown to have very hazy ideas about the difference between a letter and

a word, and neither did they understand the terms author, illustrator, title, full stop, comma and page.

Having checked the child's grasp of these fundamental concepts, the teacher may decide to try to observe how the child selects a book. Many 'late bloomers' seem to oscillate between a lack of confidence when choosing a book, which leads to them taking one which they know by heart, and taking books which are far too difficult for them to read. Selection with direction may be the answer, whereby the teacher selects around five books which she knows the child could manage and then invites the child to choose one of them.

Sometimes a child will appear to be on the verge of success but then, when offered an unknown text or something with a different cover from the series he knows, he goes to

pieces and makes wild guesses or freezes. Reading the story to the child first and ensuring he understands and enjoys the book will help to reduce his anxiety, and then using a 'paired reading' approach where the child and an adult simultaneously read the text will build up his confidence. Do not worry if the child appears to have learnt the text by rote, but praise his delivery and then select a few words or a sentence from the book and let the child practise reading these, perhaps offering them as part of a game. (See Chapter 4, 'Developing a sight vocabulary'.)

Some children acquire a small sight vocabulary but almost refuse to look at any new vocabulary, waiting for the teacher to provide the word. A

strategy for tackling unknown words is essential for all readers, as the ultimate aim is to enable the child to read without any adult help. In order to encourage the child to apply this strategy automatically, it is necessary to ensure that all adults with whom the child reads select the same procedure. The strategies which the teachers decide are best for the children will undoubtedly vary from school to school and from child to child. However, the procedure is likely to encompass some of the following points.

• The child is encouraged to read up to the word again at speed from the beginning of the sentence.

• The child is encouraged to miss out the word and continue reading the sentence.
• The child is encouraged to 'sound out' the first letter or digraph of the word.
• The child is encouraged to 'guess' once more, drawing on all available cues, including picture, meaning and sound.

One school successfully used the following strategy. Children were given two envelopes, one labelled 'difficult words' and the other labelled 'words I know'. The teacher noted down any word the child found difficult in the book he was reading and wrote these words on to small pieces of card which were placed in the first envelope. The child was then encouraged to practise reading these words, either through games or by reading to his parents from the

same text. The child was encouraged to ask the teacher to 'test' him at any time, both by reading the book which contained these words and finally by recognising them in isolation. Every word that the child read successfully went into the envelope marked 'words I know' and was proudly shown to the headteacher and parents. This approach could obviously be adapted to encompass letter sounds, letter formation, words and sentences.

In order for the 'late bloomer' to thrive in Y3 and not become disillusioned and worried about reading, careful records need to be provided for the new class teacher so that the progress continues. This will ensure that the child is not presumed to be able to tackle texts for which he is not quite ready. (See Chapter 14, 'Using parents wisely', and Chapter 15, 'Assessing reading'.)

ACTIVITIES

1. Alligator appetite

Age range
Six to seven.

Group size
Twos and threes.

What you need
Card, a pen, scissors.

What to do
Cut up some card to make playing-card sized pieces, and on each one write a word. Make sure that each player has at least three copies of each word. The object of this game is to try to make the child quickly identify basic sight words. It may be necessary to start with only three or four words (such as 'here', 'I' and 'am') and gradually build up to ten.

Ask the group to sit round a table, then turn over all the cards so that the players can see them. Read all the words to the children and check that they can also recognise them.

Tell the children that you are a hungry 'word alligator' and that you are going to gobble up all the words. Explain that the children must try to stop you.

Ask one of the children to call out one of the words that are on the table. When she does so, encourage the rest of the children to start to pick up as many of the cards showing the word as they can. Count to five under your breath and then also grab as many cards with that word on them as possible.

Let a second player select a word to call out and continue playing until all the words have been taken from the table.

The winner is the player with the most cards.

Once the children understand the game, let them take turns at being the 'word alligator'.

2. Bingo match

Age range
Six to seven.

Group size
Five children.

What you need
Card, a pen, a highlighter pen, scissors, pencils, an eraser.

What to do

The object of this game is to consolidate knowledge of letter names, sounds and formation.

Select five letters you wish the group to practise. For example, choosing c, a, d, g and o would allow the players to practise the 'c' family. Other letter combinations could be:
• i, l, w, m, n (starting with a down stroke);
• g, p, j, y, q (letters below the line);
• k, b, h, l, t (tall letters).

Cut some card into squares, then write each letter on to a separate piece. Mark the top of each card to ensure that the caller holds up the card correctly. Make 'bingo' cards for each player, filling in three different letters for each

Figure 1

board, but ensuring that no letter appears more than three times. Write these letters using the highlighter pen and show their position in relation to the line, as well as indicating the starting place with a dot, as in Figure 1. Ask four of the children to be players and the other to be the caller.

Give each player a board, and ask the caller to shuffle the cards and place them face down on the table. Let the caller pick up a card and show it to the players, reading out the letter name if they can. Explain that any player who has this letter on his bingo card may write over the letter with a pencil. Ask the caller to watch and make sure that the players start from the dot.

Continue play in this way until a player has completed all the letters on the card, when she should call out 'Bingo!'. Ask the player to say the name and sound of the letters on her card. If she gets this wrong, play continues.

3. True or false?

Age range
Six to seven.

Group size
Two to three children.

What you need
Copies of photocopiable page 183, scissors, card, adhesive, felt-tipped pens, a die, counters.

What to do
Make a baseboard by drawing a sequence of brightly coloured squares, each one numbered. Cut up a copy of photocopiable page 183 along the lines, then write true or false on the back of each strip as appropriate.

Place the sentence strips face upwards beside the board, then let the children roll the die in turn. Allow the child with the highest score to start the game by rolling the die and moving his counter the corresponding number of squares. If he lands on a coloured square, ask him to pick up the first sentence strip, read it out and say whether this is 'true' or 'false'. Let him turn over the strip to check if he has decided correctly. If so, let him move on three squares and roll the die again. If incorrect, the player should stay on the square and the next child can roll the die. The winner is the child who reaches 'home' first.

4. Silly or sensible?

Age range
Six to seven.

Group size
Two to three children.

What you need
Copies of photocopiable page 184, scissors, card, adhesive, felt-tipped pens, a die, counters.

What to do
Make a baseboard as described in the previous activity. Cut up a copy of photocopiable page 184 as indicated, then write 'silly' or 'sensible' on the back of each strip as appropriate.

Place the sentence strips face upwards beside the board then let the children roll the die in turn. Allow the child with the highest score to start the game by rolling the die and moving his counter the corresponding number of squares. If he lands on a coloured square, ask him to pick up the first sentence strip, read it out and say whether this is 'silly' or 'sensible'. Let him turn over the strip to check if he has decided correctly. If so, let him move on three squares and roll the die again. If incorrect, the player should stay on the square and the next child can roll the die. The winner is the child who reaches 'home' first.

5. Who am I? What am I?

Age range
Six to seven.

Group size
Two teams of two.

What you need
Copies of photocopiable page 185, scissors, thin card, adhesive.

What to do
Cut up copies of photocopiable page 185 and stick them on to pieces of thin card. Shuffle the cards and lay them face down in a pile on a table.

Let one pair pick up a card and read it to the opposing team. Ask the second team to try to guess who or what is being described. If they can guess the answer, let them keep the card. If they do not get the answer, place the card at the bottom of the pile.

Let the pairs take turns at asking questions until all the cards have been won. The winning team is the one with the most cards.

Further activity
Let the children make their own clue cards based on this game.

Our cat wears glasses when she reads the newspaper.

CHAPTER 14

Using parents wisely

'Teachers should take account of the important link between home and school, actively encouraging parents to participate and share in their child's reading'. (DES/WO 1989b.)

Most teachers are firmly convinced that the best learning environment for a child is one where there is a partnership between home and school. Gone are the days when there was a white line on the playground which indicated 'No Parents Past This Point'. The Government has emphasised the importance of parental involvement in schools, and many parents are eager to play a full role in their child's education.

Obviously there are many ways of involving parents in the life of the school and the education of their children. What works successfully in one school might be inappropriate and unpopular in another. Nevertheless, there are some important issues to be addressed if a school is to use parents wisely. One important issue is the involvement of parents in a school reading policy.

BACKGROUND

A home-school reading policy

Research has shown the importance of parental involvement in children's reading (Tizard et al, 1981). Some schools have been running parent partnership schemes for many years. Other schools use the scheme in certain classes but not uniformly throughout the school. Others still do not have any formal policy for involving parents, although parents do support their children's reading on an informal basis.

The advantages of a home-school policy

The advantage of formalising home-school reading practice into a policy is that it gives it status in the eyes of parents and teachers. Moreover, it enables the policy to be reviewed and refined in the light of experience. If a policy runs smoothly, so that parents easily become familiar with it and new teachers are quickly able to participate in it, there will be the continuity of approach which is so important for children's success.

If books are sent home by one teacher and not sent home by another teacher in a parallel class, then parents can understandably be confused about the importance of the practice. A clear policy provides guidelines for parents and teachers and ensures that systematic support is offered to all children.

Communication

If parents are to play a satisfactory role in their children's reading success, then the school needs to explain to them how reading is taught and how they can participate. For example, teachers see a wordless book as an opportunity for the child to interpret pictures and to weave her own narrative stimulated by the pictures. Many parents would be unaware of the relevance of looking at a wordless book as a necessary step towards understanding how stories work, how ideas connect and how plots develop. Teachers need to share their expertise with parents so that parents understand why certain things are done in certain ways in school.

The communication between parents and teachers is too often a one-way conversation with the teachers telling parents what goes on in the classroom and what they should do at home, without allowing any opportunity for parents to share their own knowledge about their children's reading. Parents have expertise about their own children and teachers have expertise about children in general. What is needed is a pooling of this expertise. Communication between home and school needs to be a dialogue, with parents contributing as well as learning from the staff.

How to communicate a school reading policy to parents

There are many ways of communicating information to parents. Some parents respond well to written communications, while others rarely respond unless they have been approached personally; some parents welcome a quiet talk with a teacher on a regular basis,

others would be unlikely to attend such sessions; some parents enjoy a public meeting, while others would find such a form of communication daunting. It is important that different styles of communication are explored to discover which ones reach out most effectively to all parents.

An outline of precisely what the school expects parents to do to support their children's reading development is too important to be left to just one form of communication. It will almost certainly require small group meetings of teachers and parents with a follow-up booklet. An attempt will also need to be made to track down those parents who did not attend the small group meeting. All this takes time and effort, but as this home-school partnership has proved so vital in children's reading

success, it is too important to offer it only to a minority of parents.

What do teachers expect parents to do?

'There is no doubt whatever of the value of the parent's involvement in the early stages of reading. What needs careful thought is the nature of that involvement and the attitude they bring to it.' (DES 1975.)

It is important that a school makes clear to parents what they can do in order to assist their child with reading. Some parents will automatically take

on the role of 'teacher'; other parents will decide that teaching the child to read is the teacher's job. The kind of help teachers will want parents to provide will depend upon various factors:

• the child's age;
• the difficulty of the book chosen;
• who chose the book – teacher, child or parent;
• the child's stage of development;
• the child's level of confidence.

All these matters need to be sorted out initially by the members of staff and their intentions need to be communicated clearly to parents.

Should the school send books home?

All the evidence shows that a considerable number of homes have very few books for adults, let alone any suitable books for a beginner reader. Thus if schools do not send books home, many parents will not be able to be involved with their child's development as a reader.

To suggest that all parents make use of a local library is neither practical nor realistic. Of course, being a member of a library and choosing books to share together at home is a delightful way to widen a child's interest in reading, but it might be a luxury that many parents would find too difficult to provide. Even when a trip to the library does not incur expensive travelling costs, problems can still await parents at the library as they are unlikely to find it easy to choose books that their child can read. The truth is that if the school does not provide books for sharing at home then many parents will be unable to provide suitable reading material.

Core reading schemes

If teachers decide to send home books from the core reading scheme, they may hit upon several problems.

• Scheme books are clearly labelled with their level of difficulty, and it is very easy for a parent to believe that this is the most important feature of a book, irrespective of the child's interest in the content. This can encourage parents to force children through the scheme. Scheme books also make available to all parents information that a teacher would use discreetly and professionally but which might not be handled so sensitively at the school gates ('I see your Jack is still on blue level. My Amy finished them ages ago'). Competition between parents can only be harmful to a child's confidence and progress.

• If scheme books are sent home they may not all be returned promptly, and this may cause problems in the classroom organisation of books.

• If scheme books are sent home, the parent's expectation will be that the child *should* be able to read it. This can put an unfair burden upon children and make them reluctant to read at home.

• By their very structure, scheme books demonstrate the extent of children's reading ability. However, while reading from them, the child is bound to make mistakes in the process of learning. Mistakes might be miscues to the ears of a teacher who intends to use the information professionally; they can be twists of a knife in a parent's heart. It is better to send books home so that children can excel in their parent's eyes. It can be disappointing to feel that one has not performed well for one's teacher; it can be disastrous to fail in front of one's parents.

• If a child reads the same scheme book at home as she does with the teacher at school, problems can arise when the child claims to have finished the book at home. The teacher is then faced with the dilemma of whether to accept the child's word and offer another book, or question the child's word and ask him to re-read a few pages. This testing can be demoralising for a child, and reading out of context can detract from the emphasis in the classroom on sustained reading.

The above objections are not intended to imply that it is *always* wrong to send scheme books home. However, they do indicate that there are many important issues to be addressed before a school embarks on this practice. Such decisions need to be made by all the staff, taking into consideration the particular needs of the school.

Which scheme books should I send home?

Some schools keep a selection of books specifically as 'going home' books. This takes the pressure off books needed for classroom use, but to have a supply of books specifically for this purpose can be an expensive solution. Perhaps the best compromise is to have a wide range of books available for children to take home, including picture books, library books and information books, as well as reading scheme books.

Obviously, not all children will be able to read every kind of book, so teachers will need to indicate to parents what kind of support a child will

need with any particular book. For example, the teacher could have three sets of bookmarks, each with one of the following messages marked on it:
• Please read this book *to* your child.
• Please read this book *with* your child.
• Please *listen* to your child reading this book.

This indicates to parents the nature of the help required and should avoid the problem of parents trying to persuade their five-year-old to read the encyclopedia she borrowed from school because she saw some pictures in it that looked exciting!

Sorting out bookmarks each day is not a lengthy process, and children are soon able to make these decisions for themselves.

The home-school notebook

Some schools send home notebooks in which the teacher makes suggestions as to how parents can best help their children. The notebook allows parents to respond, commenting upon their child's enjoyment of the book or mentioning any difficulties found. Children can also be encouraged to make comments about books they have read. An over-elaborate system that involves the teacher in making lengthy comments for each parent each day is too time-consuming, but, used wisely, this system can be an important channel of communication, particularly if parents have any anxieties. The notebook can also be used by the school to remind parents of events (for example, swimming on Tuesday; meeting at school tonight, and so on). Of course, for children in Y2 it is perfectly reasonable to let them write these

messages themselves as this provides them with a real audience and purpose for their writing. Furthermore, this increases the likelihood of the message getting home when the child wishes to show off his writing skills!

Losing books

It is impossible to ensure the safe return of all books which are sent home. Some books will get lost. Hopefully this loss can be offset against the benefits of a successful home-school reading partnership. However, certain practical procedures can help to keep tabs on books.
• Send books home in plastic zipped wallets. These have the advantage of protecting books which might fall into puddles on the way home, and they are also more conspicuous in a busy household than a slim paperback book.
• Encourage parents to return books to the classroom in the morning or after school. When this becomes part of the routine for parents, they not only start to assist in the selection procedure, but also share the responsibility for the safe return of books.
• Always praise a child who returns a book which you thought had been long lost. If you make accusations you will deter anyone else from returning a book found under the bed three months later.

Involving parents

'We hope parents will share books with their children from their earliest days, read aloud to them, and talk about the stories they have enjoyed together. Reading is best

taught in the classroom when teachers build on this basis.' (DES/WO 1989a.)

It is perfectly true that some parents do become very fraught if their children do not make good progress in reading. Moreover, as some parents' definition of 'good progress' is frequently an impossibly high standard it might be tempting to leave them out of the equation altogether. However, this would hardly solve the problem. Such parents are going to behave in this way whether you provide books from school or not.

The important thing is to recognise that this is a potential problem with certain parents and to anticipate this by educating them as much as possible. For most parents, the time of maximum anxiety about progress is at the early stages of reading. It might be advisable to direct parents to support their child's reading at this stage by reading *to* their child. However, this can only be successful when parents have had explained to them the advantages of reading to children. The school should stress the following points.

• Reading to children does not make them lazy about reading. On the contrary, it shows them the advantage of being able to read and enjoy such books for oneself.

• Reading to children demonstrates all the conventions of reading that are just as important as word recognition (anticipating the plot; reflecting upon the action; poring over the illustrations; following the line of print; turning the pages).

• Reading to children provides a role model of adults reading

– a situation which is not easily replicated on other occasions in our busy lives. Most children do not see their parents regularly engrossed in books and consequently start to get the impression that reading is something that adults keep telling you is great but which they themselves rarely do.

Once parents are convinced that in being asked to read *to* their children, they are not being fobbed off with an unimportant aspect of their children's reading progress, but rather are being offered a valuable complementary role to the teaching of reading in the classroom, many will relax and enjoy this important stage in their children's development.

Parental help in the classroom

Of course parents need not be restricted to helping their own child at home. Many parents have the time and enthusiasm to offer their services in the classroom. Usually this help is

very welcome and many schools have come to rely upon small groups of parents who regularly spend some time in school. If this help is to be to the best advantage of both pupils and teachers, parents should be carefully guided as to the sort of help they can provide.

Some schools encourage parents to hear children read. However, unless the school has spent considerable time and effort in preparing parents for this task, this may not be the most appropriate support for them to offer. Hearing children reading in the classroom offers a teacher the opportunity to make all sorts of judgements about a child's progress, such as informally analysing miscues or assessing a child's interest in a particular book. If a parent hears a child read, all that valuable diagnostic information is falling on deaf

ears. It might be better to take advantage of parents helping in the classroom by directing them to read *to* children, either individually or in small groups. Many early years teachers bemoan the fact that they do not have enough time to read stories to children. The pressures of the curriculum mean that the number of occasions when a teacher can spend time with a small group of children reading a story, discussing the pictures, and chatting about what went on in the story, are very few indeed. Parents in the classroom can help to increase the number of those important book sessions.

Parents can also help in the classroom by playing educational board games with small groups of children. Again, this is something on which class teachers probably wish they could spend more time. An extra adult in the classroom could make it possible.

Teaching parents to help their children

We should not be surprised that some children have difficulties in learning to read. Considering the complexity of the task, it is remarkable that so many children become readers so quickly!

Despite all the work of the experts, we still do not know precisely how children learn to read. However, although we may not have definitive answers about what guarantees reading success, we do have a fairly clear picture of what hinders a child's progress. If children lack confidence in their own ability to succeed then their chances of success are reduced. Parents have an important part to play in boosting the confidence of their children. Parents and teachers need to work together

to find ways of enabling every child to succeed. The ideal time to demonstrate to parents the best way of helping their children's reading is at a specially arranged parents' meeting.

Some schools hold meetings for parents before the children actually start school. Although this might seem to be laying the right foundations for successful partnership in the future, many parents are more concerned at this point about other questions:
• Will my child survive a whole day without me?
• Will he get to the loo in time?
• Will she eat the school lunch?
Perhaps a better time to hold a parents' meeting would be a few weeks into term, once parents have relaxed a little

about these issues and are more receptive to suggestions from staff about reading.

When should we meet?
Evening meetings might be easiest to organise, but afternoon meetings are also worth considering. Some schools hold these meetings 45 minutes before the end of the school day, with one teacher addressing the parents, one teacher running a crèche for younger siblings and two other teachers managing double groups of children. Obviously, this is quite an organisational feat, but the dividends might well justify the effort.

Whom should we invite?
Although a whole-school meeting can be an impressive show of solidarity by the staff, most parents respond better to an informal year group meeting. This enables teachers to speak very specifically about parental involvement at one particular stage. It also enables parents to contribute without feeling overawed in a room full of other adults.

How often should we meet?
Ideally, teachers should have contact with parents once a year to talk specifically about support for literacy. It is probably best to hold these meetings during the first term of each school year. Of course, this is not essential, and when a school has adopted a whole-school policy towards parents in partnership then the meetings will be part of an ongoing programme of advice and parental feedback.

What to do at the parents' meeting
It is perfectly understandable that parents want their children to succeed, but many parents want instant success. Teachers need to explain to parents that pressure from home will only hinder a child's progress. Children need support, encouragement and sympathy. Criticism and unrealistic expectations are no help at all. There is only a limited time available for communicating this to parents, so it is important that the key points of the message are effectively conveyed.

The activities in this chapter differ from the others in this book in that they are all activities for the teacher to carry out with groups of parents rather than groups of children. They are intended to give parents a greater appreciation of what it is like to be a beginning reader and an understanding of how they can best help their children.

ACTIVITIES

I. Mirror writing

Group size
Any size.

What you need
Copies of photocopiable page 186.

What to do
Distribute copies of photocopiable page 186. It is important that these are distributed quickly so that everyone is looking at the text at the same time.

Ask the parents to read the writing, stressing that they may not hold it up to the light and read it from the back. After a few minutes, ask the parents about their reactions. For example:
• How did they feel looking at a page of print that looked vaguely familiar but which was so difficult to read?
• Would it have helped if someone had said 'sound it out'?

• Were they anxious that other parents in the hall seemed to be better at reading it?
• Did they use their fingers to 'keep their place'?
• Did they read it aloud?
• Can they remember what the writing was about?

This last question is very important because most parents will be surprised to discover that they have not paid any attention to the meaning of the writing.

Suggest to the parents that this exercise replicates what their children might be feeling when faced with a page of print.

If some parents have read the page by holding it up to the light and reading it from the back (despite the fact that

you told them not to!), remind them that for their children there is no magical way to make the words in a book instantly readable.

Two important lessons should emerge from this exercise. Parents are reminded that:
• reading is not an easy task;
• if when we are reading, we are too busy decoding (that is, making up the words from their constituent sounds) it becomes very difficult to hold on to the meaning of what we are reading.

2. What do we read?

Group size
Any size.

What you need
No special equipment.

What to do
This activity can help parents see the importance of reading in all our lives. Reading is not only about becoming engrossed in a work of fiction. Reading is part of being a member of our society.

Ask parents what reading they do each week. At first many parents will say that they haven't enough time for reading. However, if asked to examine their week more closely, they will realise that they are doing some kind of reading each day. This could include reading letters, cereal packet offers, television advertisements, Teletext, advertising fliers, television listings, newspapers, recipes, magazines, hobby books, knitting patterns, notes from school, calendars, shopping lists, labels on tins, parking tickets, train and bus timetables...

3. Choosing reading material

Group size
Small groups.

What you need
A selection of picture books.

What to do
A greater awareness of the criteria used when selecting books will help parents to understand better how and why their children make choices about books.

Provide the group of parents with a selection of picture books and ask them each to choose one. After they have chosen, ask the parents what attracted them to that book. Lead this gently on to a discussion about how we choose books and how children choose books.
• Did they choose something that looked familiar?
• Did they choose something that looked easy?
• How do they choose books and magazines for themselves?
• Do they like certain books for certain occasions, such as a romantic story for a holiday read or the book of a serial on television?

4. Aspects of reading

Group size
Small groups.

What you need
A selection of picture books, copies of photocopiable page 187.

What to do
Ask the parents each to choose and look at a book. (Some will feel more confident if they share the reading of their chosen book with a friend; some may choose to read silently.) When everyone has finished reading, ask them to talk about their book. Many parents will undoubtedly be hesitant to speak out in such a situation, so take care to guide them. Make comments and observations to demonstrate that the questions are not tests about ability to read or ability to find hidden meaning in books, but simply to react to ideas, words or pictures in the book.

Remind parents of the obvious pleasures of sharing a book with others. Many of them will have enjoyed telling the group about a funny incident or illustration in their book. Their children, too, should have this opportunity to share the pleasures found in a book.

Using one of the picture books, show the parents how much we can learn from looking at the pictures. As adults, we become so accustomed to making pictures in our heads by reading the words that we frequently ignore the pictures, or just glance at them briefly. This tendency to hurry past the pictures may take away from children many of the pleasures of reading picture books and, as parents, we can be re-educated into a picture-literate world.

Ask parents if they can remember learning to read. Many will not be able to remember in much detail. Ask them why they think this is so. Others will have clear memories of happy or sad occasions when becoming a reader. Use this talk to lead into a discussion about what helped us become readers and what might have been unhelpful.

Distribute copies of page 187 for the parents to take home with them. This provides a checklist of ways in which parents can help prepare children to become readers.

5. Reading role-play

Group size
Any size.

What you need
Help from another teacher, copies of photocopiable pages 188 and 189.

What to do
With another teacher, demonstrate the techniques of hearing a child read, one teacher playing the part of the parent and one pretending to be a pupil. This style of presentation will be most effective if you first demonstrate what parents should *not* do. This could include:
• choosing a time for reading when the child is engrossed in a television programme;
• not paying much attention to the child or the book;

- showing by one's body language that hearing the child read is an unpleasant duty;
- getting cross each time the child stumbles over a word;
- telling the child always to 'sound out' unfamiliar words;
- offering no words of praise or support.

Obviously for the entertainment of the parents this scenario can be 'hammered up' to exaggerate all the things done incorrectly. This is quite important as some parents might feel a little guilty if they have been doing some of the things demonstrated. However, it is unlikely that any one parent will have been doing everything wrong. This mixture of guilt and self-satisfaction creates a good atmosphere for conveying the important messages about helping at home.

After this demonstration of how not to do it, demonstrate a successful home reading experience. This should include the following aspects:
- a sensible time is chosen for reading to take place;
- the parent looks at the book, talks about the story and chats with the child;
- the parent constantly praises and supports;
- the parent encourages digression from the text to allow the child to discuss the pictures, or comment on the story so far.

This visual demonstration of helpful techniques can often be much more convincing than reading out a list of dos and don'ts. However, the demonstration can be reinforced by distributing copies of photocopiable pages 188 and 189, which offer basic guidelines for parents. Included with these is advice to parents on the subject of paired reading, together with an explanation of the concept.

6. Recording reading

Group size
Any size.

What you need
Cassette recorder and tape or video camera and player, books.

What to do
Before the parents' evening, make some recordings on a cassette tape or video of a

teacher hearing a child reading in the classroom.

Play the recording to the parents, making sure you stop the tape frequently to highlight features of good practice to parents who would otherwise be unable to identify them clearly.

Conclude the activity with a general discussion. Do the parents have a greater appreciation of how best to help their children with their reading? Do they feel more confident? What further help do they feel the teacher could give?

CHAPTER 15

Assessing reading

Teachers have always recognised the need to keep a record of what a child has read and over the years numerous systems have emerged. The question we need to consider is whether record-keeping systems can be useful when assessing how *children read*. For example, recording only the book title and the number of pages read does not give any indication of how a child reads. Indeed it can create an impression, both for the child and for others involved in helping him read, that reading is a linear process and that the sole purpose of reading is to 'get through the book'.

Of course, it is necessary to record what children read. By doing this it is possible to monitor choice and help children extend their range of reading. However, if we are to understand reading and reading development, any recording system must include some form of assessment.

Where previously we may have recognised the strategies that children use when they read to us or to each other, we may not always have recorded them. There follow some descriptions of types of reading assessment and suggestions for record-keeping.

ASSESSMENT

Observation

Regular and systematic observation of reading behaviour can provide useful insights into reading development. By observing and recording different aspects of a child's reading in a variety of situations over a period of time, it is possible to compile a reading profile of the child. The notes made should record what has actually been observed, and thus will provide data for a reliable and detailed interpretation of the child's reading development.

When to record

Continuous observation of reading behaviour should not be undertaken by setting aside a regular time each week in which to make notes. This is likely to provide only limited information as the child may be in a similar situation on each occasion. To be of most use, observations should be made and recorded whenever the opportunity arises. This method of assessment can be time-consuming, since it requires the teacher to observe during all reading occasions and not just when hearing a child read. However, it will provide information on:
• the range of material read;
• the strategies the child is acquiring;
• the child's strengths and weaknesses.

In addition, the record will provide more information than a simple checklist, and may be used both summatively and formatively. A summative record provides information about a child's achievement, whilst a formative record provides information that assists the teacher to plan future work.

What to observe

The following suggestions are neither definitive nor prescriptive. The most useful observations are those that are selected by the teacher and that reflect the aspects of reading behaviour which have been agreed by all the staff as necessary for inclusion in developing a reading profile.

Choosing a book
Can the child select a book:
• from a small selection?
• from a large selection?
• independently?
• with support from an adult?
    What influences the child's choice:
• the size of the book?
• the size of the print?
• the amount of illustration?
• familiarity with the characters?
• the subject matter?

Attitude to books
Does the child:
• want to read or share books with the teacher?
• want to read or share books with other children?
• ask to take books home?
• become engrossed in a book?
• talk about books?
• use 'book language' when playing or in conversation?
• make connections between different books (based on

similarity of plot, subject matter or illustrations)?
• read as a preferred activity?
• enjoy rereading old favourites?

Comprehension

Does the child demonstrate comprehension by:
• retelling what has been read (literal comprehension)?
• reading between the lines, considering possible or implied meaning (interpretive comprehension)?
• making associations with other knowledge, experience or reading (applied comprehension)?
• reflecting on what has been read and perhaps adjusting his initial responses or existing knowledge (critical comprehension)?

Strategies

Does the child:
• self-correct for meaning?
• use pictures as clues?
• use initial sounds as clues?
• use the shape of words as clues?
• use grammatical structure to predict?
• use grammatical structure to self-correct?
• indicate that correction is necessary by pausing?
• read aloud fluently and with appropriate intonation?
• appreciate the difference between reading aloud and reading silently?
• use punctuation to support meaning?
• read silently?

Knowledge about books and print

Does the child:
• hold the book the right way up?
• know that books are read from front to back?
• know the difference between words and pictures?
• know that reading proceeds from left to right?
• know that reading proceeds from line to line?
• know that words on the page represent the words that are spoken?
• appreciate that there are gaps between words?
• recognise that upper and lower case letters have the same phonic function?
• recognise that joined writing and print can convey the same message?
• understand terms such as word, letter, page, illustration, sentence, punctuation, paragraph, chapter, title, author, contents, index, glossary?

The above suggestions will help the teacher use observations made in the classroom to develop a reading profile of a child. This may be greatly enhanced by information the child's parents or guardians can supply. If possible, talk to parents about the child's reading, both at home and in the general environment. For example, ask them whether their child enjoys listening to stories, reads shop signs, posters,

television advertisements and so on. You may like to include a checklist for parents in the school's pre-school information pack.

Running records

The running record is a method of recording how a child handles texts. It helps teachers to discover how a child is developing as a reader and whether she is progressing from dependence to independence. The process is described in detail in Chapter 7, 'Hearing children read'.

Running records can be used in the very early stages of reading, when children:
• retell stories using picture cues;
• remember and draw upon some of the language of books;
• are beginning to know the difference between words and pictures;
• are beginning to understand about the directionality of print.

The running record can also be used during the gradual move towards independent reading, when children start to:
• understand word separation;
• match the spoken word to the written word;
• use initial consonants to help them tackle words;
• draw on knowledge of how words look;
• apply self-correcting strategies.

This type of analysis can supply useful insights into early reading development, and can provide a basis for planning activities to support reading. Of course, it may be that teachers feel that this form of assessment is too formal for young readers and could give children the message that they are being tested. However, if a running record analysis is undertaken once or twice a term as a matter of course, and if children are included in discussions about their reading, it can be valuable in helping them to begin to reflect on their developing skills as readers.

Published reading tests

When considering the assessment of reading, many teachers feel that using a published reading test will provide them with 'hard evidence' of reading development. Before buying a reading test, the following points may be worth considering.
• Will the test reveal anything not already discovered from other assessment methods already in use, such as observation, running records, discussion with children and/ or parents, or reading record books?
• Will the test help with planning for a child's reading development?

• Who are the results for, and how are they to be used?
• Is the 'reading ability' measurement obtained from a test the same as reading potential?
• Will the test give a balanced view of a child's reading? For example, does it refer to attitude, interest or habit? Does it give insights into the child's ability to infer and deduce?
• Is reading ability measurable?

If your school decides to use a published reading test, it might be useful to consider the following factors.
• The type of test – is it standardised or criterion-referenced? Standardised tests enable a child or group of children to be compared against an average standard. A test is standardised by testing a large group of children of a specific age and obtaining the average standard. Criterion-referenced tests measure what a child or group of children can do. These tests usually concentrate on specific skills and the results show how far these skills have been obtained. They do not compare children against a standard.

• What is the test's applicability? Is it for a group, or an individual?
• Validity – does the test measure what it is required to measure? Does the test yield consistent results?
• How should the test be administered? How can the results be used?
• Cost – are the materials consumable or non-consumable? How long will it take to administer and mark the test?
• Suitability – is the test culturally biased? Is it dated? For what age group is it intended? Does the organisation of the material reflect the reading materials that are familiar to the children?

Types of test

A range of types of tests are described below, together with some of their advantages and disadvantages.

Standardised norm-referenced reading test
Intention
The purpose of this test is to compare a child or group of children with the average standard of the country.
Advantages
A standardised norm-referenced reading test:
• can provide a system of communication between teachers throughout a school and across phases;
• shows the ability range of pupils within a class;
• can provide the LEA with information to compare school achievement throughout the country, borough or district.
Disadvantages
A standardised norm-referenced reading test:
• gives no indication of the

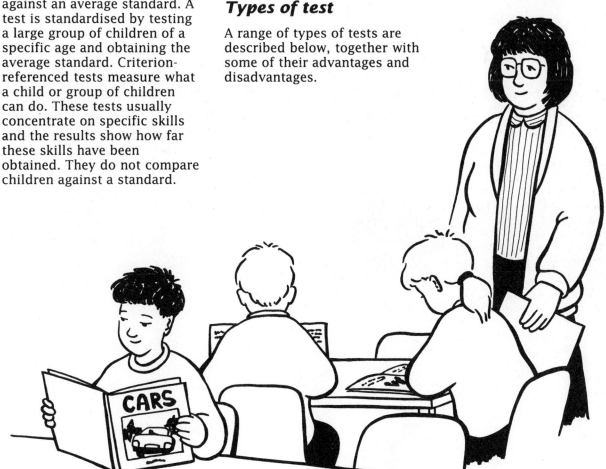

strengths of individual children;
• can rapidly become dated;
• does not usually reflect our multi-cultural society;
• does not measure attitudes to reading;
• does not often reflect current approaches to the teaching of reading.

Standard criterion-referenced test
Intention
The purpose of this test is to measure what a child or a group of children can do. It usually concentrates on specific skills.
Advantages
A standard criterion-referenced test:
• shows the level the individual child has reached in a particular skill;
• shows how many children in a class have mastered a particular skill;
• is generally easy to administer and mark;
• may provide a check for the effectiveness of a reading policy.

Disadvantages
A standard criterion-referenced test:
• applies to isolated skills and therefore does not relate to the breadth of a language policy;
• can lead to the teaching and testing of isolated skills;
• generally gives less detailed and useful analysis according to how easy it is to administer and mark;
• gives no indication of strategies that a child uses;
• gives no indication of how a class or group compares with a national standard.

Group reading test
Intention
The purpose of this test is to assess the reading ability of a group. It can be standardised or criterion-referenced.
Advantages
A group reading test:
• is generally quick to administer and mark;
• generally makes it easy to obtain a 'reading age' from the score;
• can allow for a silent read;
• sometimes covers the whole primary age range and can therefore provide a form of continuity of assessment.

Disadvantages
A group reading test:
• may intimidate children and therefore cause them to under-perform;
• usually requires written answers in the form of either multiple choice or a cloze passage;
• is often organised in such a way that children sometimes do not finish the test, with the result that they may view themselves as 'failures'.

Individual reading test
Intention
The purpose of this test is to assess the reading ability of individual children. It can be standardised or criterion-referenced.
Advantages
An individual reading test:
• enables the teacher to observe how a child approaches reading;
• generally gives a diagnostic assessment;
• is generally reusable.
Disadvantages
An individual reading test:
• can be very time-consuming;
• unless used for diagnostic purposes, gives results similar to those yielded by group reading tests (which have the advantage of being faster);
• sometimes makes it difficult to distinguish between a 'misreading' and a halting but accurate read;
• may lead to the teacher unconsciously prompting the child;
• requires oral reading which may inhibit the child's understanding of what has been read.

Phonic assessment
The methods of assessment and the checklists already described will help teachers analyse whether and to what

extent a reader is drawing on semantic and syntactic knowledge. However, they do not provide any information about a child's phonic knowledge, and therefore one of the components is missing from the picture of the child as a reader. Teachers do need to be aware of a child's phonic knowledge, as phonic knowledge will help a reader tackle unknown words. Very often an initial sound will encourage the reader to guess, and in doing this the reader is helped to draw on all cueing systems. A phonic knowledge record sheet is a useful way of assessing and recording what is known, and provides a basis for planning phonic activities.

The reading record book

Many schools have developed a record-keeping system which can be used by all those involved with children and reading. It usually takes the form of a personal log book in which all reading done by the child is recorded. The entries are usually dated and are often accompanied by a comment written by the child or the person with whom the child has been reading. The comments may refer to how the child read the book, for example, independently or with support, and/or to the child's response to the text.

This type of log is a useful addition to other methods of assessment. It provides a record of what has been read and what support, if any, was required. By referring to the log the teacher is able to see what reading preferences a child may have and to plan appropriate support. This knowledge will also help the teacher suggest other titles and authors that may interest the child, and thus help to extend his range of reading and encourage an ability to select. A reading record can also provide an opportunity to develop a dialogue with parents or guardians about how children may be helped at home. In addition, it provides the parent with an opportunity to make comments about the child's reading or to raise any concerns.

Parent interviews

A valuable insight can be gained by discussing with parents or guardians their children's pre-school experience of books and reading. For example:
• Is the child used to hearing books read aloud?
• Does the child have any favourite books, stories or rhymes?
• Does the child enjoy looking at books on her own?

This discussion could be included in the general pre-

school interview and might possibly become part of regular parent/teacher consultations. It would also provide an opportunity for the teacher to suggest appropriate ways in which the child's reading development might be supported at home (see Chapter 14, 'Using parents wisely').

Finally it is important to bear in mind that there is no one standard method of assessment that will suit all children. The way in which reading is assessed will vary according to the reading experience of the child and the reasons the teacher has for undertaking the assessment.

Assessing reading materials

Teachers are naturally concerned to assess and record reading effectively. In order to do this, it is also necessary to evaluate the material upon which we base our judgements. For example:
• Is the book interesting?
• Do the illustrations support the text?
• Does the book reflect the interests or experiences of the reader?
• Is the story worth reading?
• In the case of non-fiction, is the information accurate?

If we are to answer the above questions, we will need to consider the criteria used to select books and how those criteria were established. For example:
• Who is responsible for buying the books in school?
• Who is involved in deciding what is bought?
• What criteria are purchasing decisions based on?

As a first step in evaluating the books in school and considering new purchases, it may be helpful for staff together to develop a set of agreed criteria for choosing books. The following may provide starting points for discussion.
• Does the book portray stereotypical images of gender, race or age?
• Does it fairly represent our multi-cultural society? Is the book acceptable to all races?
• Will the book be interesting to children?
• Does the book provide opportunities to enrich the language and experience of the reader?
• Does the book look worth reading?
• Does the book provide the reader with opportunities to extend his knowledge of the world, himself or others?

Further general points to consider may include such things as:
• What is the minimum number of books that should be allocated to each class?
• Should there be multiple copies of favourite books? If so, where should they be kept?
• Is quality preferable to quantity?
• What help is available from others (such as the school library service, local library, local bookshop)?

Once the criteria have been agreed and the books have been bought, it is worth remembering that however plentiful and attractive the school or class book provision may be, the books will stay on the shelf if they are not actively promoted!

PHOTOCOPIABLES

The pages in this section can be photocopied and adapted to suit your own needs and those of your class; they do not need to be declared in respect of any photocopying licence. Each photocopiable page relates to a specific activity or suggestion in the main body of the book and the appropriate activity and page references are given above each photocopiable sheet.

Word race, page 45

Reading role-play, page 154

Books to share with your child at home

Alfie Gets in First, Shirley Hughes, Picture Lions.
And So Can I! Bill Gillham...
Arthur...

...llins.
...oks.
...n Ahlberg, Picture Lions.
...e Puffin.
...David Armitage, Picture Puffin.
...ynley Dodd, Picture Puffin.
...Picture Puffin.
...Deutsch.
...Hedderwick, Picture Lions.
...Pienkowski, Picture Puffin.
...cture Puffin.

...berg, Picture Puffin.
...gs,

Photocopiable pages 169

Space race game, page 44

Photocopiable pages 189

Photocopiable pages

Look alike, page 42

Word race, page 45

Recording phonic knowledge, page 53

Date_____ Name_____ Age_____

● Acquired letter knowledge

easily ☐   quickly ☐   slowly ☐   recently ☐   with difficulty ☐

● Plays word/sound games

enthusiastically ☐   indifferently ☐   with difficulty ☐

● Ability to work in small groups

good ☐   average ☐   poor ☐

● Ability to work from worksheets

good ☐   average ☐   poor ☐

● Ability to join in with rhymes

good ☐   average ☐   poor ☐

● Ability to retain letter/sound matches

good ☐   average ☐   poor ☐

● Uses letter/sound matches in writing

frequently ☐   sometimes ☐   never ☐

● Ability to use letter/sound match in reading

good ☐   poor ☐   never appears to use this ☐

● Comments and thoughts on further development of sounds:

Recording phonic knowledge, page 53

Phonic knowledge record sheet	Name
Knows initial consonant sound	b c d f g h j k l m n p q r s t v w x y z
Knows initial consonant name	b c d f g h j k l m n p q r s t v w x y z
Knows two-letter consonant blends	bl cl fl gl pl br cr dr fr gr pr tr dw tw sl sm sn sp st sw
Knows three-letter consonant blends	spl shr str scr spr thr
Knows short vowel sound	a e i o u
Knows long vowel sound/ name	a e i o u
Knows the sound of consonant digraphs	th sh ch wh ph gh
Knows vowel/consonant digraphs	ar or er ir ur
Knows the sound of vowel digraphs	ai ay oa ow oe oo ew ue ie ee ea oi oy ou ow au aw
Knows alphabet names	a b c d e f g h i j k l m n o p q r s t u v w x y z
Knows alphabet order	
Can match upper and lower case letters	A B C D E F G H I J K L M N O P Q R S T U V W a b c d e f g h i j k l m n o p q r s t u v w X Y Z x y z
Can form the following letters	
Can join the following letters	
Comments	

Start

Hurrah! You have won the race.

Bunny hops

a b c d e f g h i j k l m

Start

Lily pad race

n o p q r s t u v w x y z
Start

Story word squares, page 67

My word search for _____ by _____

I give this book [ ] marks out of 10

Chart of reading experience, page 103

Name _____

Type of book	Date completed				
Fiction					
Anthology					
Short story					
Picture book					
Poetry					
Story on tape					
Book from home					
Comic story book					
Non-fiction					
Dictionary					
Reference book					

How to choose a story book

1. Look at the cover. Does the book look **interesting**?

2. Look at the author's **name**. Have you read other books by this author?

3. Look at the **front** cover or the back of the book. You will find a short description of what happens in the book.

4. Read **one** page. Can you read most of the words without much difficulty?

5. **Read** the book by quickly flicking through the pages. Does it look like the kind of book you enjoy reading – not too long, not too short, with enough pictures?

6. **Make** your decision.

I
N
F
O
R
M

A flow chart for selecting information books

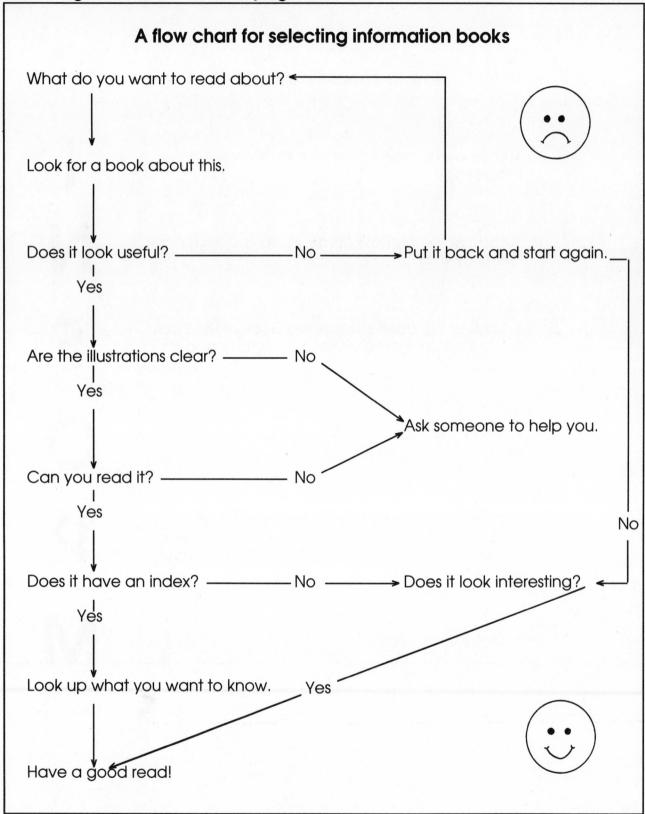

What do you want to read about?

Look for a book about this.

Does it look useful? ———————— No ————————> Put it back and start again.

Yes

Are the illustrations clear? ———— No

Yes

Ask someone to help you.

Can you read it? ———————— No

Yes

No

Does it have an index? ———————— No ————————> Does it look interesting?

Yes

Look up what you want to know.   Yes

Have a good read!

Maths (*Arthur*), page 109

Pet	How many?	Food	How much?

Dear _____ ,

Please could you come to our school on _____ at _____ . We will be talking about _____ .

Yours sincerely,

_____ .

Urdu

خوش آمدید

محترم ......

برائے مہربانی آپ بروز ...... بوقت .... اسکول تشریف

لائیں۔ ہم .... کے بارے میں گفتگو کریں گے

مخلص

Greek

Ἀγαπητοί _____ ,

Προσκαλῆστε νά ἐπισκεφθῆτε τό σχολεῖο μας τίν _____ στίς

_____ .

Θά μιλήσουμε γιά _____ .

Εἰλικρινῶς

Arabic

عزيزي ......

أرجو أن تحضر إلى مدرستنا في يوم

.... الساعة ...

وسيكون موضوع الحديث ...

المخلص

True or false? page 140

Little Boy Blue wore a red suit.	The Gingerbread boy was eaten by the wicked fox.
Old King Cole was very miserable.	The Three Bears thanked Goldilocks for eating their porridge.
The Three Bears lived in a house in the woods.	The glass slipper fitted Cinderella's foot.
Jack and Jill carried water in a paper bag.	Hansel and Gretel enjoyed living with the witch.
Snow White stayed in the house with the seven dwarfs.	Little Bo Peep lost her feet.
Little Red Riding Hood liked visiting the wolf.	Jack stole the hen from the giant.

Silly or sensible? page 141

Mum always puts the butter in the oven to keep it cool.	The tree fell over in the storm.
Dad likes to clean the car with paint.	The owl saw the mouse run under the hedge.
The cat purrs when she's happy.	If you run very fast you will fly.
Our fish can sing 'Baa Baa Black Sheep'.	Our dog wags both his tails when he is upset.
The cat next door barks at dogs.	My sister walks on her hands so that her shoes won't wear out.
Our cat wears glasses when she reads the newspaper.	Fish like walking on grass.
We don't go to school on Sundays.	My friend caught the boat at the bus stop.
Dad wears his glasses so that he can see through the wall.	Dad takes the dog for a walk in the kitchen.

Who am I? What am I? page 141

I am made from wood. I have four legs. You eat your meals off me. I am a ... table.	You can take me to the beach. I have a handle. You can fill me with water. I am a ... bucket.	I have green scales. I frighten people. I can breathe fire. I am a ... dragon.
I am made from wood. I have a black or coloured centre. You write with me. I am a ... pencil.	I come in a pair. I am very sharp. I can cut paper. I am a ... pair of scissors.	There are three in our family. We live in a wood. We like eating porridge. We are the ... Three Bears.
I fly in the wind. You hold me with string. I sometimes have a tail. I am a ... kite.	I have a screen. I have a keyboard. I help you to write. I am a ... computer.	There are three in our family. We like to eat grass. We know how to trick trolls. We are the ... Three Billy Goats Gruff.
People like my smell. I am a flower. My stem has thorns on it. I am a ... rose.	I am seen in the sky. I can make shadows. I am a star. I am the ... sun.	I have two sisters. I work very hard. I lost my slipper at midnight. I am ... Cinderella.
I am shiny. I am sharp. I help you to eat. I am a ... knife.	I have four legs. I have a long tail. I purr when I'm happy. I am a ... cat.	I have a talking cat. I heard the bells ringing. I became Lord Mayor of London. I am ... Dick Whittington.
I have two wheels. I travel on roads. Children sometimes ride me. I am a ... bicycle.	I get out of breath. I like eating pork. I sometimes huff and puff. I am a ... wolf.	I am a spider. I play tricks on people. I can change my shape. My name is ... Anansi.

A reading experience

We should not be surprised that some children
have difficulties in learning to read. In fact,
considering the complexity of the task, it is
remarkable how many children become readers
so quickly!
Despite all the work of the experts, we still do not
know precisely how children learn to read.
However, although we may not have definitive
answers about guaranteed reading success, we
have a fairly clear picture about what hinders a
child's progress.
If children lack confidence in their own ability to
succeed, then their chances of success are
reduced. Parents have an important part to play in
boosting the confidence of their children.
Parents and children need to work together to
find ways of enabling every child to succeed.
After reading this, you may have some
appreciation of the difficulties many children
experience when they are asked to read
something that is too difficult for them.

A checklist for parents

• Read to your child as often as possible.
• Say nursery rhymes with your child and encourage him/her to learn them by heart.
• Point out print all around your child (street signs, shop names, advertisements and so on).
• Try to watch television with your child so that you can talk about it together afterwards.
• When possible, buy books for your child. Owning a book can be a particular pleasure. Jumble sales and second-hand book stalls are a very useful source of cheap books.

No dogs allowed in the park

• Let your child see you reading books, magazines and newspapers.
• Make full use of the local library. Choose some of the books and let your child choose others.
• Say the alphabet with your child.
• Encourage your child to 'pretend' to read, repeating the words he or she has heard you read and turning the pages at the right time.
• Enjoy this early stage of reading with your child. Happy confident children are more likely to go on to be successful readers.

Reading with children

• Read the story straight through. Occasionally you can make a comment, such as 'I wonder what will happen next?' or 'Oh no! Look at what the naughty puppy has done'. Sometimes you can run your finger underneath the line of print, showing your child that the words that you are saying are the ones on the page.

• Occasionally you can say 'Turn to the next page. I have finished reading all the words on this page.' This helps your child to realise how we go about the process of reading.

• If you have time, reread the story, stopping often to discuss both the story and the pictures with your child.

• Encourage conversation. Let your child talk about the story and make connections between the story in the book and his or her own experiences. For example, 'Wouldn't it be funny if we had a magic car like that?'

• Encourage understanding. Ask your child some questions about the story. These questions are not intended as tests but to encourage your child to understand what is going on in the story. Let your child ask you questions too.

• Encourage careful observation. Ask questions which require your child to look carefully at the illustrations for the answers.

• Encourage imagination. Before you turn to the next page, ask your child what he or she thinks will happen next.

• Remember, you do not have to do all of the things in this list every time you share a book with your child, but if you can sometimes spare the time to do some of these things, you will be giving your child a good start to becoming a reader.

Paired reading

What is paired reading?

Paired reading is when you and your child read the same book together. Your reading will support your child and give him or her confidence. As the reading progresses, your child might like to read for a short time on his or her own. If he or she comes to an unknown word, read the word aloud and continue to read along together until your child feels able to try again to read alone.

What to do

• Choose a time for paired reading that suits both you and your child.

• Sit close to your child. Your child should hold the book.

• Spend a few moments talking about the book by way of introduction. Talk about the illustrations or the author.

• Start reading together. At first this might seem strange for both of you, but you will get used to it. You should read at a pace only slightly slower than your normal reading pace. Do not slow down for your child. The idea is that your child will try to keep up with you. If your child lags behind, encourage him or her to skip a few words and to look for (and possibly point to) the section you have got to. Then he or she can join in with you again. When you come to an easier part, such as a repeated refrain, your child should nudge you to indicate that he or she would like to try to manage the reading alone. Allow your child to do this, but be prepared to join in if he or she gets into difficulties.

• When you have finished reading, talk to your child about the book – did it end as he or she expected? Were there any funny parts?

• Praise your child for effort as well as success.

Books to share with your child at home

Alfie Gets in First, Shirley Hughes, Picture Lions.
And So Can I! Bill Gillham, Methuen.
Arthur, Amanda Graham, Picture Puffin.
Best First Book Ever, Richard Scarry, Collins.
The Big Sneeze, Ruth Brown, Beaver Books.
Each Peach Pear Plum, Janet and Allan Ahlberg, Picture Lions.
Going Shopping, Sarah Garland, Picture Puffin.
Grandma Goes Shopping, Ronda and David Armitage, Picture Puffin.
Hairy Maclary from Donaldson's Dairy, Lynley Dodd, Picture Puffin.
How Do I Put It On? Shigeo Watanabe, Picture Puffin.
Janine and the Carnival, Iolette Thomas, Deutsch.
Katie Morag and the Tiresome Ted, Mairi Hedderwick, Picture Lions.
Meg on the Moon, Helen Nicoll and Jan Pienkowski, Picture Puffin.
Mr Gumpy's Outing, John Burningham, Picture Puffin.
Mr Magnolia, Quentin Blake, Picture Lions.
Mrs Plug the Plumber, Janet and Allan Ahlberg,
   Picture Puffin.
The Mother Goose Treasury,
   Raymond Briggs, Hamish Hamilton.
Nini at Carnival, Errol Lloyd,
   Picture Puffin.
Our Dog, Helen Oxenbury,
   Walker Books.
Peace At Last, Jill Murphy,
   Picturemac.
Rosie's Walk, Pat Hutchins,
   Picture Puffin.
Teddy Bears ABC, Susanna
   Gretz, Picture Lions.
The Very Hungry Caterpillar,
   Eric Carle, Picture Puffin.
What Colour? Fiona
   Pragoff, Victor Gollancz.
Where's Spot? Eric Hill,
   Picture Puffin.

England and Wales

The chart on this page refers to the reading component of the National Curriculum for English. Use this chart to identify the chapters that contain activities to support each statement of attainment. There are no activities in chapters 7, 14 and 15, and so these have not been included in the chart.

Level	Chapter	1	2	3	4	5	6	8	9	10	11	12	13
1	a	●	●									●	●
	b	●	●		●	●						●	●
	c	●	●	●			●	●		●			●
	d	●		●			●	●	●		●		
2	a	●	●		●		●					●	
	b		●										
	c		●	●	●	●				●	●		
	d	●							●				
	e	●		●			●		●			●	
	f					●				●			
3	a							●		●			
	b							●		●			
	c	●		●					●				
	d							●	●		●		
	e	●				●							
	f					●					●		

Scotland

The chart on this page refers to the reading component of the Scottish curriculum for English language. Use this chart to identify the strands covered by the activities in this book. Activities are identified by their chapter and activity numbers; for example, **4**/1 means Chapter 4, activity 1. In Chapter 11 the activities are arranged in seven sections which are identified by the letters - A for *Arthur*, V for *The Very Hungry Caterpillar*, S for *The Sandal*, O for *The Owl who was afraid of the Dark*, P for *Peepo*, TL for *The Three Little Pigs*, and T for *Titch*. Thus P4 means activity 4 in the section on *Peepo*.

Level Strand	A	B	C
Reading for information	**2**/1-12, **4**/3-7, **6**/3, **8**/3, **11**/A1, **11**/S1-3, **11**/O 1-3, **11**/P 1-2, **11**/TL 2-4, **11**/T 3-6, **12**/1-7	**6**/3, **11**/A 1, **11**/S 1-3, **11**/O 1-3, **11**/P 1-2, **11**/TL 2-4, **11**/T 3-6, **12**/1-7	**6**/3, **11**/T 6
Reading for enjoyment	**1**/1-3,7, **3**/1-5, **4**/1-7, **6**/5,7, **9**/1-3, **11**/V 3, **11**/T 7, **12**/1-5	**6**/3, **11**/A 1, **11**/S 1-3, **11**/O 1, **11**/O 3, **11**/P 1-2	**3**/2-5
Reading to reflect on the writer's ideas and craft	**1**/2-6, **3**/1-4, **6**/1-6, **8**/1-7, **11**/O 2, **11**/P 4-5, **11**/TL 1, **11**/TL 6, **11**/T 1	**3**/1-4, **6**/1,2,4-6, **8**/2,4,6, **11**/O 2, **11**/P 3-4, **11**/TL 1, **11**/TL 6, **11**/T 1	**3**/2-4, **6**/6, **11**/T 1
Awareness of genre	**3**/1-5, **6**/4, **8**/2,3,7, **11**/O 2, **11**/P 4-5, **11**/TL 1, **11**/TL 5-6, **11**/T 6-7	**3**/1-5, **6**/4, **8**/2, **11**/O 2, **11**/P 3-4, **11**/TL 1, **11**/TL 5-6, **11**/T 6-7	**3**/2-5, **6**/4, **11**/T 6
Reading aloud	**1**/1-8, **3**/4, **9**/1-3, **11**/T 7, **12**/7	**9**/3, **11**/T 7, **12**/7	
Knowledge about language	**1**/8, **3**/2, **5**/1-7, **6**/1, **8**/4,6,7, **11**/TL 5, **11**/T 2, **12**/4,5, **13**/1-5	**6**/1, **8**/4,6,7, **11**/TL 5, **11**/T 2, **12**/4,5	

Bibliography

Adams, M.J. (1990) *Beginning to Read*, MIT Press.

Awdry, W. (1952) *Gordon, the Big Engine*, Kaye and Ward.

Bond, G. and Dystra, R. (1967) 'The co-operative research programme in first grade reading instruction', *Reading Research Quarterly* 2, 5-142.

Bryant, P.E. and Bradley, L. (1985) *Children's Reading Problems*, Blackwell.

Carle, E. (1970) *The Very Hungry Caterpillar*, Hamish Hamilton/Picture Puffin.

Chall, J.S. (1967) *Learing to Read: The Great Debate*, McGraw Hill.

Chambers, A. (1991) *The Reading Environment*, Thimble Press.

Department of Education and Science (DES) (1975) *A Language for Life* (The Bullock Report), HMSO.

DES (1988) *Report of the Committee of Enquiry into the Teaching of English Language* (The Kingman Report), HMSO.

DES (1990b) *Standards of Reading in the United Kingdom*, HMSO.

DES (1990a) *The Teaching and Learning of Reading in Primary Schools*, HMSO.

Department of Education and Science/Welsh Office (DES/WO) (1988) *English for Ages 5 to 11*, HMSO.

DES/WO (1989a) *English for Ages 5 to 16*, HMSO.

DES/WO (1989b) *English in the National Curriculum*, HMSO.

Dolch, E. and Bloomster, M. (1937) 'Phonic Readiness', *Elementary School Journal* 38, 201-205.

Downing, J. (1963) *The Downing Readers, Revision Book A*, Initial Teaching Publishing Company.

Gattegno, C. (1970) *Words in Colour*, Educational Explorers.

Glynn, T. (1980) 'Parent-child interaction in remedial reading at home', in Clark, M.M. and Glynn, T. (Eds.) *Reading and Writing for the Child in Difficulties*, Birmingham Educational.

Goswami, V. and Bryant, P. (1990) *Phonological Skills and Learning to Read*, Erlbaum.

Gray (1979) 'Reading progress in English infant schools; some problems emerging from a study of teacher effectiveness', *British Educational Research Journal* 5, 2, 141-157.

Hatcher, P. (1991) 'Overcoming early reading failure by integrating the teaching of reading and phonological skills: the phonological linking hypothesis', unpublished PhD thesis, Department of Psychology, University of York.

Holdaway, D. (1979) *The Foundations of Literacy*, Ashton Scholastic.

Hutchins, P. (1976) *Don't Forget the Bacon*, Bodley Head/Picture Puffin.

Hutchins, P. (1968) *Rosie's Walk*, Bodley Head/Picture Puffin.

Krashen, S. and Terrell, T.D. (1983) *The Natural Approach: Language Acquisition in the Classroom*, Pergamon Press.

Martin and Brogan (1972) *The Teacher's Guide to the Instant Readers*, Holt, Rinehart & Winston.

Milne, A.A. (1928) *The House at Pooh Corner*, Methuen.

Minghella, A. (1988) *The Storyteller*, Boxtree/TVS.

Morris, J.M. (1974) *Language in Action*, Macmillan.

Smith, F. (1978) *Reading*, Cambridge University Press.

Southgate, V., Arnold, H. and Johnson, S. (1976) *Extending Beginning Reading*, Heinemann Educational.

Tavener, D. (1985) *Children Reading to their Teachers*, National Association for the Teaching of English.

Tizard, B., Mortimore, J. and Burchell, B. (1981) *Involving Parents in Nursery and Infant Schools: A Source Book for Teachers*, Grant McIntyre.

Williams, J. and Ackerman, M. (1971) 'Simultaneous and successive discrimination of similar letters', *Journal of Educational Psychology* 62, 132-137.

Yopp, H.K. and Singer, H. (1985) ' Toward an interactive reading instructional model', in Singer, H. and Ruddell, R.B. (Ed) *Theoretical Models and the Process of Reading*, International Reading Association.